D1412686

Musk Mania

HANS VAN DER LOO & PATRICK DAVIDSON

Musk Mania

Elon Musk's five insane principles of success

First published by Vakmedianet in 2017.
This edition published by Maverick House in 2018.

© 2016 Vakmedianet, Deventer – Hans van der Loo and Patrick Davidson
Translation © 2017 Niels Stegeman
Cover design: Vivianne Smiggels
Graphic Design: Hans Roenhorst, H2R+
Text editing: Isabel Timmers
Translation: Niels Stegeman

6 7 8 9 10

Maverick House,
Unit 33, Stadium Business Park,
Ballycoolin, Dublin 11,
Ireland.
D11HY40

www.maverickhouse.com

info@maverickhouse.com

A CIP catalogue record for this book is available from the British Library.
ISBN: 978-1-908518-59-0 (hardcover edition)
ISBN: 978-1-908518-61-3 (ebook edition)

The paper used in this book comes from wood pulp of managed forests.
For every tree felled, at least one tree is planted, thereby renewing
natural resources.

Content

For Sebas, Joran and Casper

Do what makes you happy. This will provide you with energy.

Do it often. You'll become good at it eventually.

And then you can make the impossible come true.

Not because you have to, but because you want to.

Hans and Patrick

June 2016

Foreword

Deeply impressed. That's how I felt when leaving the Tesla factory in Fremont, situated on the other side of the bay of Silicon Valley, after visiting them for an article for NRC Handelsblad. A glittering white factory where people worked, supported by bright-red state-of-the-art robots, on producing Tesla's electric luxury saloon, the Model S. At the rear of the factory was a conveyor belt, where owners could take delivery of their personalised car, cheering loudly while doing so.

I visited the factory in early 2013. Only several thousand Teslas had been sold by this point and it was still completely unclear whether or not consumers dared the transition to electric cars. And yet, it quickly became clear to me that something extraordinary was going on here. Here were thousands of employees working on and believing wholeheartedly in the mission of founder Elon Musk: the car of the future is sustainable, luxurious, sexy and exquisite in every single way. All details were pointed out to me at an unrelenting pace and with unbridled enthusiasm: the enormous touchscreen! The boot at the front, where normally you find the engine! And of course the incredibly powerful battery that allows the car to go from stationary to 100 kilometres per hour in 5.6 seconds!

Such infectious excitement about a product I had only seen previously with regards to Apple products. Elon Musk has therefore been designated the successor to Steve Jobs by Silicon Valley. Where Jobs reigned over Apple, Musk heads no less than two companies: Tesla and aerospace company SpaceX. Aside from ushering in a revolution in the area of sustainable energy, Musk also wants to colonise Mars, should the Earth ever become uninhabitable.

Realising big dreams, that's the central theme of Elon Musk's life. At first glance, Musk's ambitions seem the dreams of little boys: fast cars and rockets. But those boyish dreams are driven by a much more expansive vision. You'll read it later on in this book.

We often snigger at such far-reaching vistas in the Netherlands. Nonetheless, it's worth your while to delve into Musk's philosophy. He not only has the biggest ambitions, but he's also quite adept at realising a fair number of them. Just look at Tesla: shortly after my visit, the American Consumer Organization declared the Model S the best car ever made.

Elon Musk is a Wavemaker, or so write Hans van der Loo and Patrick Davidson. With a clear-cut vision, daring, willpower and the ability to move the people around him, he's changing the world. How it works exactly is something you'll read in this book. Because even if you can't run two businesses at the same time nor prefer dying on Mars, Elon Musk is someone who can inspire you to pursue your dreams. Using Musk's lessons, Hans and Patrick will show you: everyone can make the difference in the things we do.

Eva de Valk,
Tech journalist and author of Silicon Valley

Introduction

'Hey guys, I think we can build

this rocket ourselves.'

Elon Musk

Elon Musk, the ultimate Wavemaker

On 1st April, 2016, thousands of people are waiting in line all across the world to buy a car that only exists on paper. For a thousand dollars, they can consider themselves the virtual owner of an electric car which will be delivered in one to two years: the Tesla Model 3.

A few days later, Tesla starts operating the Gigafactory. This gigantic battery factory produces innovative batteries that are three times stronger and better than any available thus far. When the factory is in full swing, that differential should increase even further. And making Tesla the largest producer of batteries in the world. The latter is mostly a pleasant side effect. The factory is mainly a profit machine. The dream of a sustainable world is foremost. Tesla even makes the blueprints of the factory public, so that others can also work on the dream of sustainability.

A few days later, for the first time in history, the American company SpaceX succeeds in landing a rocket on a so-called drone ship floating in the sea. An expert said the achievement was comparable to 'shooting a pencil across the Empire State Building during a storm, and to then have it land on a shoebox'. The video images appear to show a 'normal' rocket launch, just in reverse. In the middle of the sea, a towering, slim rocket is flawlessly parked on the deck of a ship. Ready for the next return trip. Because that's what it's all about: reusing a rocket should become just as easy as starting your car.

The ultimate Wavemaker: dreamer, thinker and doer

Three amazing achievements in one week. With the same man as the driving force: the South African-born Canadian-American Elon Musk. Inventor, entrepreneur, investor and world-improver. The man who blazes into hermetically-sealed worlds and then proceeds to knock everyone off their feet with his achievements. Only few succeed as a newcomer in the automobile industry in gaining a foothold. With his Teslas, Musk unleashed a whirlwind revolution in the field of electric driving. His aerospace company SpaceX, with its recyclable and affordable rockets, competes successfully with the substantially closed-off bastions of NASA, Boeing, Lockheed Martin and the Russians.

During our intensive quest for Wavemakers (do read on to find out what we mean by that), Musk popped up again and again. To us, he is both the embodiment of and something larger than a Wavemaker. Musk is much more than just an inventor, entrepreneur and investor. He doesn't just thrive on the waves of change, he succeeds in creating waves himself. How incredible his ideas may sound, he sees opportunities to realise them. How? By following his heart and doing what he truly wants to do. To be fair, there are more people who do that. But Musk also possesses phenomenal mental and imaginative powers, which make him see what others pass by. Add to that the guts to admit his breathtaking ambitions, the ability to make his dreams work for him, the strength to work for ten or maybe even 100 and the talent of drawing the greatest talents to him. Because Musk leaves the execution of those plans to people who believe in them just as strongly as he does. He demonstrates how you can change the world by yourself. By instigating a wave of renewal and taking others with you.

You either love him or hate him

Some find Musk's plans a little over the top. Others even call him megalomaniacal and reprehensible. As is often the case with outspoken personalities: you either love him or hate him. That first group is growing fastest. Everywhere he comes, people flock: officials considering him to be a new source of employment, managers who bask in his prophecies of the future and the general public, who can't get enough of his sayings and inspirational stories. Musk fires revolutionary idea after revolutionary idea at us—new methods for generating energy, a hypersonic means of transportation, and a new way to dig tunnels. And more: he delivers as well.

Getting into the mind of Elon Musk

In this book, we'll expose the five guiding principles of the success of Wavemakers in general and those of Elon Musk in particular. Let's not pretend Elon Musk is an unwritten page, however. An extensive biography appeared in 2015. Thousands of blogs and videos circulate on the internet. He's been the subject of hundreds of articles. And yet, we still meet people who've never heard of him or can only name a few superficial facts: 'Oh, that's the guy with those electric cars' or 'Isn't that the weirdo who wants to go to Mars?'

Aside from quick and easy access to the wondrous world of Musk, you'll get the chance to get into his mind. Learn from him. Think big. Dare. Persevere. Be a Wavemaker. In your own way. There are few people who can or dare do what Musk does. And that's just fine. But in a time where the waves of renewal are churning and slamming into each other, it's imperative you light the flame of renewal within yourself.

When asked, only 20 per cent of the Dutch employees say they consider themselves an instigator of change. That must mean 80 per cent does not. We hope that reading this book will give you that spark. Let Musk be an example in allowing the Wavemaker principles to set your imagination on fire. And then take the step from dreaming and thinking to doing: use the principles to increase your own freedom of movement and achieve that which you deem unthinkable.

The five principles of making waves

1. Offer hope in fearful times
2. Be aware of all things
3. Aim for Mars
4. Play to win
5. Move people

To make a truly world-changing wave, a personal touch is a key ingredient. For Elon Musk, it's his exceptional personality profile and the unique combination of dreamer (vision), thinker (scientific reasoning) and doer (entrepreneur). No less important is the fact that he's driven by a kind of primal force. This is what we mean with 'mania'.

Meet Elon Musk and learn how he applies the five principles of the Wavemaker in his own inimitable way.

The reasonable man adapts himself

to the world.

The unreasonable one persists in

trying to adapt the world to himself.

Therefore all progress depends on

the unreasonable man.

George Bernard Shaw

1

The turbulent world of the Wavemaker

'I think it is possible for ordinary people

to choose to be extraordinary.'

Elon Musk

A half-naked boy dances on a hilltop. As he demonstrates the wickedest moves, a second dancer joins in. And another. Eventually the group of trendsetters is joined by an ever-increasing crowd of enthusiasts and before you know it, the hill has been transformed into a mass of dancing people. One lonely dancer who manages to get an entire crowd going... it seems like magic. And yet it isn't. It's the power of the Wavemaker.

Traditional leaders set out a stable course in an atmosphere of security and trust. But in these times of transience, insecurity and complexity, there is ever more a need for momentum as opposed to stability. For leaders who are quick to rise to action and are continually on the move. For people who thrive on waves, but also cause them. These are Wavemakers. Wavemakers are game changers, hope bringers, a driving force and disseminators. They break up existing structures and certainties and create new possibilities. They always look ahead, offer perspective and hope in fearful times. Not by looking at what's going wrong, but by seeing what's possible. They don't just inspire, but are also a driving force, people who aren't afraid to put themselves out there and work passionately on realising their often sky-high ambitions. They do today what is needed tomorrow. This makes Wavemakers the driving force behind a plethora of new initiatives, new ideas and behaviours that spread across the globe en masse and as quick as can be. They have great influence on how others think and act. Including you. They thrive in a turbulent world. And they also keep that turbulence going. Because they know: when the waves are in, they are in.

'Wavemakers do today what is

is needed tomorrow.'

Tidal waves

If you know how it works, you can recognise the set roles, principles and patterns governing the creation and growth of movements. This applies equally to heady waves at sea and to ideas, behaviours, feelings, opinions and products. Or viruses. Just as one person becoming ill can start a flu epidemic, one person thinking differently can dislodge all encrusted axioms. Or one new invention that shakes the world at its very core. The pattern is always the same: it starts off small and grows and grows until it reaches massive size. And this is how one person is capable of setting off gigantic tidal waves. Elon Musk is a Wavemaker who knows how to cause tidal waves.

Wavemakers come in all shapes and sizes. Wavemakers are usually individuals, sometimes form a small group and very occasionally a full-sized organization or agency. Often, they are people with a small-scale, temporary impact. A very literal example can be seen in a stadium, where a lone person suddenly gets up off his seat and brings both arms up and down. Before you know it, a whole stadium is participating in his 'wave'. Another example: someone starts applauding loudly at a concert or a speech, and moments later the whole room breaks out in applause. The impact of these types of waves is limited. Both with regard to time (it'll calm down a few moments later), to scale (no one gets affected outside those present) and to effect (normality soon reasserts itself).

There are also Wavemakers who make true tidal waves. Tidal waves can sweep away in a matter of moments all that has been previously and painstakingly constructed. Roads and buildings, but traditions and winning formulas as well. At the same time, they create space for renewal. Elon Musk is a Wavemaker who knows how to cause tidal waves.

Musk Mania: maniacally positive

He even stands at the cradle of a veritable Musk Mania. We mean two things by this. For starters, the maniacal fashion in which Elon Musk leaves his mark on the world. It's not just done with exceptional passion and enthusiasm, but at an astounding pace. The terms maniacal and mad are often used with regards to being mentally ill. We see maniacal and mad in a positive light: to us, these terms refer to passion, intractability and enthusiasm. And even if there are dark aspects to his character, Elon Musk is mostly maniacally positive. A modern and restless redeemer who wants to offer new hope to a torn and rampaging world. A positive remedy

21

against feelings of apathy and fatalism, he wakes people up and gets them moving.

'Musk Mania' doesn't just refer to the maniacal tendencies of the man himself, but also to the phenomenal impact he currently has. Elon Musk is nearly singlehandedly capable of continually controlling the media channels, get dignitaries and investors to lose their senses and tempt consumers into irrational behaviour. Like that purchase of a not-yet-produced car. Elon Musk is the half-naked dancer who gets the crowd moving. But then on an epic scale. Manic scenes we know, at sporting matches and with pop stars. The incredible images of the Beatles in the 1960s were already termed Beatlemania. Nowadays, Bieber has his Beliebers. And racing talent Max Verstappen is also in line to develop a Max Mania. Musk makes this happen, too—and then some. He's capable of capturing masses of people. People who want to be close to him and be a part of his success. But it's mostly people who want to believe in him: Musketeers, and more than just three.

2

The flight of Elon Musk

> 'Starting a company is like eating glass
> and staring into the abyss.'
>
> **Elon Musk**

Elon Musk's life reads like a three-part book for boys. It begins with his 'flight from Africa': after a difficult start, Musk leaves South Africa at age 17. Nearly broke, he travels to Canada and leaves for the United States a little later. There commences the second act of his life story, the 'flight forward': after his studies, he makes millions as a fledgling entrepreneur in Silicon Valley. The third and, for now, final act of his life, is the 'flight upwards'. Literally and figuratively. Musk conquers space, but also works away on solutions in the field of sustainable energy.

The flight from Africa: no match with his environment

Elon Musk was born on the 28 June 1971, in the South-African city of Pretoria—the eldest in a family of three: his brother Kimbal and his sister Tosca. Mother Maye, once contender for Miss South Africa, is still active as a model, into her sixties. She also runs a dietary practice. Father Eroll owns a successful engineering company. The family does well financially from the get-go, but the interrelationships are stormy. When Elon is roughly six years old, his parents decide to separate. Maye leaves with the children for the holiday home in Durban.

Two years later, Elon makes the surprising decision to move back in with his father. Surprising, as his mother said they got along well, but also because his father exhibited quite dominating and manipulative behaviour. 'It would certainly be accurate to say I did not have a good childhood', Elon later says. 'It was like misery. He's good at making life miserable—that's for sure.' His brother Kimbal would later add: 'He definitely has serious chemical stuff [imbalances]. Which I am sure Elon and I have inherited.' Elon suffers even further from his social surroundings, more so than from the unstable home situation. South Africa has a strong macho culture, one of tough guys with big mouths and typical male mannerisms. There is no room there for a dreamer with a nerdy look. The young Musk is also a classic know-it-all who corrects everyone. It doesn't endear him to his peers, who prefer pulling pranks or sports He's teased and regularly beaten up. It's no wonder he later described his youth as 'non-stop horrible'.

His only solace is reading about inventors, futuristic worlds in galaxies far away and new machines and technologies. After school, he 'lives' in the local bookstore, where he disappears into the world of science fiction, fantasy and comic books. This way, he not only shuts out the big bad outside world, but grows even smarter. The young Elon seems at times lost in a trance. He gets this typical, distant look in his eyes. Anyone who talks to him can't seem to get through. This happens so often, his parents suspect him of being deaf. 'He goes into his brain, and then you just see he is in another world', says his mother. 'He still does that. Now I just leave him be because I know he is designing a new rocket or something.' This quality makes him even less popular at school than he already is: his absence is interpreted there as arrogant and somewhat deranged.

From a young age, Musk was an introvert thinker and dreamer. But was he already a doer? Not at school, if we're to believe his teachers and classmates. He may have been smarter than the rest, but does little with those smarts. This changes when, at age nine, he sees a computer in an electronics store. 'It was like, "Whoa, holy shit!". I had to have that and then hounded my father to get the computer.' The computer came with a manual with enough material for six months. It takes Elon three days and nights to master it. His new hobby also gives him his first financial gains. At age 12, he sells the software of his first videogame to a magazine. It earns him 500 dollars.

The combination of computer knowledge and the commercial possibilities the surging internet offers are the key to the second episode of Musk's life: successful entrepreneurship.

The flight forward: study and start-ups

Elon and South Africa do not get along. Even in his early teens, he dreams of leaving for the States, the land of boundless opportunity. As his mother is of Canadian descent, that country becomes a first stop. The urge to escape his early environment regardless of the cost must have been strong, for Musk leaves for Canada practically unprepared. He knows of a vague great-uncle in Montreal, hops on a plane and hopes for the best. On arrival, his great-uncle has turned out to have moved long ago. With no more than 100 dollars in his pocket, Elon has only himself to rely on. Through scattered relatives all across the country, he finds shelter and several badly-paid jobs. When his mother, brother and sister also decide to travel to Canada, the family is reunited in Ontario, where Elon enrolls at university.

In 1992, when Musk is 21, he gets a scholarship to the University of Pennsylvania and leaves for the United States. Once there, he asks himself the question of how he can have the most impact on improving the world. His list: internet, sustainable energy and space travel. He would systematically take up all these subjects in the years to follow.

In 1994, Elon and his brother make a road trip which takes them to Silicon Valley. The positive energy that prevails there, the sky-high ambitions that continually enflame people and the freedom to do whatever your mind thinks of: it moves them so much, the brothers decide to return the next summer. After Elon's graduating, it even becomes their home base.

Elon's attempt to get a job at the incredibly popular internet company Netscape fails: he walks in unannounced, waits rather clumsily in the lobby and is too shy to speak to anyone. He leaves matters unfinished.

Time for plan B: Elon and his brother found the internet company Zip2 together, publishing a kind of Yellow Pages online. No very sensational, but important for their first experiences as beginning entrepreneurs. It's a classic tale of burning the midnight oil while under great pressure and with no penny to spare, to force the desired success. Elon especially has it rough, when investors sidetrack him due to a lack of leadership abilities. The pain is compensated in the end when then-computer giant Compaq takes over the company for a staggering 307 million dollars. And 22 million dollars of that amount goes to Elon Musk's bank account. Only 27 years old and already a member of the select group of dotcom millionaires.

Taking his earned riches and enjoy life to the fullest and relax? Not Musk. He's already set his sights on a new venture: an online bank. Thanks to an internship with a large bank, he purports to know that bankers are usually rich and

> 'Musk doesn't gamble,
>
> but systematically realises his dreams.'

complacent. Musk wants to wake up the financial world with an internet bank and deal with internet inefficiency. The result: PayPal. The company grows fast, but behind the scenes a huge battle of egos is being fought. Once again, Musk's personality encounters quite the resistance from partners and investors. In a quite uncivil manner—Musk has only just left on his honeymoon when he gets the news—he's sidetracked by them. While he remains one of the biggest owners, he has little to say on the direction the company goes in. Musk remarkably lays low. An attitude that is rewarded in 2001 with an amount of 180 million dollars, when eBay takes over the company.

The flight upwards: beyond the stars

By then, Elon Musk has grown to be one of the most successful icons of Silicon Valley. For Musk, it's the moment to put the pedal to the metal and dare to fly upwards. The money he earns with selling his start-ups is almost immediately invested in a new aerospace company, in a small producer of electric cars and in a company that makes solar panels. His friends say it's an impulsive gamble. But Musk does not gamble. He's systematically and level-headedly working on realising his dreams. Those dreams have been relegated to the background in the previous years, what with all the demanding work. Now, with the confidence of a universally-celebrated entrepreneur and with sufficient resources to not be directly dependent on others in order to realise his dreams, Musk focuses on the vision from his teenage years, when he dreamt of spaceships that took people to other planets. Not a luxury to Musk, but a dire necessity. Due to the depletion of natural resources and the dangers of a possible nuclear war, humanity has little other choice than to one day pack its bags and move by rocket to other places in the universe.

Musk is officially still employed at PayPal as an advisor when he revives his aerospace plans. His friends in Silicon Valley are not quite sure how to deal with it. 'When he was talking about space, I figured he was talking about office space,' says one of them. Others have more interest in a successful IPO or other ways of making a financial landslide. To Musk, this latter fact is an indication that Silicon Valley is not quite the right place for him. He feels that entrepreneurs there lack grand ideals and far-reaching ambitions, in order to have a lasting impact. They stubbornly cling to the internet. To Musk, it's only a waystation. His destination is space.

To get there, he firstly decides to move to Los Angeles. There he can surround himself with world-class aerospace specialists, to refine his ideas. He joins a local network of aerospace enthusiasts and is immediately noticed by his insistent manner in asking questions. A prominent member: 'He didn't know a lot about space, but he had a scientific mind.' Together, they developed a vision in 2001, Mars Oasis: transport a small greenhouse with seeds to Mars, supply them with water and thus enable life on the red planet.

As NASA had no plans to explore Mars in the future, Musk decided to take matters into his own hands. He travels to Russia several times to purchase a number of cheap missiles, but ends up going home empty-handed each time. The team returns home discouraged and indulges in quite a few alcoholic beverages on the flight back. Except for Elon Musk. He works on his laptop, turns around and shows a spreadsheet. 'Hey guys, I think we can build this rocket ourselves.' For months, he's absorbed all the important knowledge of space experts like a sponge. As per usual, he's devoured dozens of books, only to discover that rockets can be manufactured much more cheaply.

He contacts several fanatical aerospace engineers. An old warehouse in a Los Angeles suburb is transformed into a production facility and headquarters. The employees' desks are scattered throughout the factory, so that everyone— including Musk—can be easily approached and contact one another directly.

Shortly after embarking on his space adventure, Musk decides to pump a substantial part of his money into another revolutionary project: the production of cool, electric cars. With his company, Tesla—named after one of Musk's great examples, the famous inventor Nikola Tesla—he sets himself up as a champion for beautiful and fast cars based on sustainable energy. The strategy is to put electric cars on the map in three steps. First, the development of a luxury electric sports car, to prove that electric cars can be cool. Then, a luxury saloon to compete with prominent brands such as BMW and Mercedes. And for a current encore: the production of a cheap, electric car for the general public. The money that's left was invested in SolarCity in 2006, a company specialising in the production of solar panels, which is run by his two cousins. By the end of 2016, Solar City is incorporated into Tesla Motors, which is rechristened as Tesla, an integrated energy company which not only produces cars but also batteries and products for energy generating.

Now, the creation of a new car concept and getting rockets into space might be less easy than you would think. In 2008, critics and sceptics seem to be in the right faster than they'd have thought. Not just the rocket launches turned out to be complete failures, the luxury sports car, too, is described in the media as the biggest high-tech failure in history. Furthermore, the world economy collapses and the auto industry is hard hit. Musk's funds are rapidly shrinking. His personal life is not fairing any better. His marriage to his college sweetheart Justine fails and ends in a fierce divorce battle, one the media is eager to report on.

Then, the fourth rocket launch succeeds and NASA closes a billion dollar deal with SpaceX for the supply of its space stations. Later on, SpaceX is the only one that succeeds in sending rockets into space and having them return neatly to Earth. This cuts costs in half and makes it much cheaper to send freight, scientists and even tourists into space in the future.

Even since that fourth successful launch, Elon Musk has had everything going for him. What's more, it seems that, after getting over his low point in 2008, everything he touches turns to gold. But luck is made. Especially if your name is Elon Musk and you keep believing in your dreams. Even at the worst of times, the thought of bailing out and selling his companies doesn't even occur to him. This demonstrates so much resilience, fortune finds you again, seemingly of its own accord. That's when you have the ability to make a shining future.

3

Elon Musk: rarely boring?

'Once you figure out the question,

then the answer is relatively easy.'

Elon Musk

'His achievements are quite something, but my God, that man is boring', one Dutch reporter laments after reading Musk's biography. He's not alone in using that word, next to descriptions ranging from crazy to genius. But what do you expect of the man who works more than 16 hours a day, who has neither the time nor the inclination for in-depth interviews and who also wants to review and correct everything that's noted down? That alleged dullness most of all has to do with his personality type. A type that also ensures that special combination of thinker, dreamer and doer.

Elon Musk is an INTJ. This is a four-letter code of the Myers-Brigg Type Indicator, one of the world's most frequently used tools for mapping out personality profiles[1]. Those letters stand for: Introversion (I), Intuition (N), Thinking (T) and Judgment (J).

INTJs are also called Scientist, Analyst or Mastermind. We prefer using the latter term: Mastermind with a capital 'M'. Because to INTJs, life is an abstract puzzle that requires solving. They are true Masterminds: thinkers with a great deal of imagination. They think independently. They're curious, decisive and ambitious. But they are also closed off and introverted. Masterminds only sparingly put effort into social contacts.

Due to their inherent thirst for knowledge, Masterminds are often called bookworms when they're little. And while this is mostly not meant as a compliment, they will probably wholeheartedly agree. Because they themselves greatly enjoy their broad and in-depth knowledge. These Masterminds firmly believe that everything is possible. As long as you have sufficient knowledge and dedication. To them, most people are too lazy, short-sighted and egotistical to fully realise their potential. Those who cannot keep up with their thinking prowess and tempo or worse, don't see the point, won't be able to count on much sympathy or respect. Also, Masterminds are usually ardent gamers, who can be completely immersed in a game of World of Warcraft, FallOut or BioShock. That's right, a few of Elon Musk's favourite video games.

---

1   MBTI is based on the work of Carl Jung and has four opposite dichotomies. The first is Extraversion (E) versus Introversion (I): do you obtain energy and information from your surroundings and other people or more from your own ideas and thoughts? The second dichotomy is Sensing (S) versus Intuition (N): are you primarily focused on concrete facts or the use of those facts and correlations between varying facts? The third dichotomy is Thinking (T) versus Feeling (F): do you make decisions based on logic and objective facts or do you let emotions be your main decisive factor? The fourth and final one is Judging (J) versus Perception (P): are you guided by lists and plans or do you take an improvisational take on things? Your final score after a list of questions consists of four letters that tell you a great deal about your character and personality.

Unorthodoxly forceful

Masterminds exude self-confidence. Their sharp talent for observation, creativity and formidable logic makes them forceful personalities. They never take accepted reality for granted. Rules, limitations and traditions are unacceptable to this personality type. Masterminds work to create the world, as they envision it.

While their ambitions and decisiveness can sometimes come across as impulsive to others, Masterminds always act as rationally as possible. However much they impassionedly work towards their end goal, they always keep a cool head while going about it. This mechanism is not only applied to work processes, but also to people. Typical human tendencies, such as informal conversations and a pleasant atmosphere, are of little meaning to Masterminds, who strive for truth, depth and perfection. They live their lives as if they're on an enormous chessboard and constantly moving pieces. Their

'Masterminds are thinkers, dreamers

and doers all in one.'

mastermind enables them to learn at an astounding rate. With care and intelligence, they stay one step ahead of others when it comes to new tactics, strategies and contingencies. This way, they keep control of the situation and ensure they have sufficient room to move about.

Nerd, visionary and entrepreneur

Masterminds are first and foremost nerds, who overthink everything and think up all kinds of things. They are furthermore visionary revolutionaries who chase after their dreams and ambitions. The emphasis on thinking and dreaming could make them very ineffectual people. But there is a third component that prevents this from happening: the urge to actually put into practice that which they've thought of and dreamed about. The Masterminds are thinkers, dreamers and doers all in one. An incredibly strong combination of a nerd, a visionary and an entrepreneur.

Masterminds easily switch between small details and the bigger picture. Their knowledge is based on idiosyncratic and often original and abstract visions and thoughts, between which they often make surprising connections. It's as if some graphics card in their brain allows them to think completely visually. On the other hand, they have a preference for tried principles and corroborated facts. Their way of thinking is evidence-based and not built upon intuitive presumptions. This makes Masterminds critical and to the point: they have an inclination to constantly check all information that reaches them. And the solution they come up with is always crystal clear. At least, in their eyes.

For example, as a child, Musk thought up a solution to no longer be afraid of the dark. 'Darkness is just the absence of light,' said the young Musk, in which he described darkness as 'the absence of photons in the visible wavelength—400 to 700 nanometers'. And who's afraid of an absence of photons?

One more thing: people with an INTJ profile are rare: it's at most two per cent of the population. A slightly larger number of men than women are Masterminds. You then try finding like-minded types who can equal the constant tendency to overthink everything and figure everything out. This makes Masterminds the absolute loners, who do their own thing. That others consider them boring, is something they take for granted. Fun fact: Musk's big example, Nikola Tesla, was also an INTJ.

A small nuance

Just to be clear: personality profiles are nothing more than a useful way of mapping out human preferences and behaviours and to accentuate them where necessary. Their purpose is not to pigeonhole someone. Personality profiles are furthermore not exclusively congenital and most certainly not unalterable. Psychologists assume that 30 to 40 per cent of behaviour comes from genetic factors. Sixty to 70 per cent has to do with learning processes and environmental influences. This means you can still refine and change your profile.

Personality profiles teach you what you're dealing with in a general sense. How a person's 'inner life' looks like, can only be determined by observing someone up close and in detail. That's why, in the previous chapter, we firstly breezed through Elon Musk's life. Now that we know what Musk's life looks like and roughly know what motivates him, it's time to dig deeper and see how he works as a Wavemaker. In the following chapters, we'll discover this by way of five success principles.

4

Principle 1:
Offer hope in fearful times

'If something is important enough,

even if the odds are against you,

you should still do it.'

Elon Musk

What is it that makes a Wavemaker like Elon Musk so different from others? He offers hope in fearful times. He shows you that today's problems are a stepping stone to a new and better world. He does this from a sense of enthusiasm, optimism and self-confidence. And from the realisation that the hope he holds out can make the difference. Offering hope is the first principle of the Wavemaker.

'Hope is the joy you experience through the expectation that the future will be positive,' said the philosopher Spinoza. Hope is more than a dream. Hope is the belief that your dream will become reality. One day. Soon. As long as you make sufficient effort to realise that hope. Hope springs eternal: it's an inexhaustible source of energy. Once seized by hope, you can wander the desert for years, in the most inhospitable of circumstances, without losing faith and becoming exhausted when things aren't looking up.

Whoever hopes, focuses on something that is about to become reality. Hope bringers help in this regard. They enthuse you into action and stimulate an optimistic view of matters. They provide you with positive energy, open the windows and tell you your desired future is already out there, that your ideal is within reach. They stimulate you into action—by yourself, but also with others. Hope bringers make you feel like you can make the difference. This makes your self-confidence grow, and by extension, your willingness to act. Even, or perhaps especially, in times of dissatisfaction and insecurity. For hope starts with the realisation that the world is far from perfect. Hope bringers show it's not only preferable, but also possible to say goodbye to what is past. They place themselves on the frontline of the change leading to a new world. This is precisely what Elon Musk does. This makes him one of the most powerful hope bringers of our times.

Visionary hope

Musk teaches us that only a clean break from the past and fundamental invigoration in our thinking and acting can lead us to a different and better world. This is the essence of visionary hope. It has its roots in the Enlightenment of the 17th and 18th centuries. The Enlightenment thinkers made a radical break from the messianism of Christian religion, which had dominated until then. Hope was no longer based on the 'soft' expectation of a vague afterlife, but on the hard 'certainties' of modern science. Thanks to science and technology, the future would be within grasp. Despite the fact that visionary hope bringers have found little support for a long time, their influence is now rapidly gaining. In and around Silicon Valley, the Mecca of digital technology, you have the so-called techno-utopians. In their eyes, technology is the answer to all human and societal issues. They place themselves at the head of a movement of world-changers and saviours of humankind. One of their most prominent members? That's right, Elon Musk.

Musk's visionary hope is based on the following suppositions. The encroaching shortage in fossil fuels can significantly break us in the future. Therefore, there is but one solution: bet everything on sustainable energy. This will most likely not save us in the end. 'If we don't ensure the creation of civilisations of multiple planets, we expose ourselves to possible natural disasters and run the risk of our civilisation going extinct,' Musk poses soberly.

To Musk, this is the only way of saving humankind. And it's not just a recent fancy of his. The fact that he was bullied as a child contributed early on to the idea that there was something wrong with the world. His love for SF and fantasy gave him the early idea that it was possible to escape the angry world.

The power of combined hope

If he had 'only' been a visionary hope bringer, Musk would probably not have made it this far and instead become a guru who sells books and gives readings. But his hope-giving qualities extend far further. Musk is also an inventor. And inventors offer hope through their cleverness and creativity. They create a new and hopeful perspective. With the motto 'If you can imagine it, you can create it,' they come up with viable solutions for the future. Technology takes centre stage herein. Reusable rockets, electric cars and high-performance batteries: they are the tangible proof that Musk isn't just spouting hot air. This comes with another quality which offers hope. Musk is also able to market incredibly desirable products. It makes him, aside from a visionary and inventor, an extremely successful and balsy 'serial' entrepreneur. He's not afraid of locking horns with the powers that be, pressing on where others stop. He raises the bar to dizzy heights. And if things are on the down, he goes that extra mile further. He's the living example of the idea that people are not the playthings of external factors or natural forces, but that everyone is capable of seizing their own opportunities and finding their own way. Whereas most hope bringers are fine with being either a visionary or an inventor or an entrepreneur, Musk effortlessly combines these three qualities. It makes him a combined hope bringer. It's no coincidence that Musk is enormously popular among millennials and even ranks above Obama as a hope bringer.

Positive emotions as a source of hope

Hope is nurtured by positive emotions; they move us. Something touches or inspires you. You want something badly or you find something very beautiful. Hope bringers, too, are led by positive feelings. It's not the same thing as, say, whooping and running over a bed of hot coals or looking at the world through rose-colored glasses. Positive emotions have much more to do with feelings of autonomy, self-confidence, optimism and enthusiasm. You won't have to look far to see these emotions in Musk.

Autonomy: he didn't get it from a stranger

His autonomy cannot be doubted: he's obstinate, easily swims against the stream, chooses his own goals and keeps his hands free to realise those goals as he sees fit. In every way, Musk is in control of his own life. Everything he does, he does with himself at the helm. This is partially handed down genetically. His mother was an example of a self-sufficient woman, capable of making her own way. Her father, Elon's grandfather, Joshua Haldeman, was an independent and eccentric man. The crisis in the 30s lost him his farm, after which he had a nomadic life wandering around, working on a construction site and as a rodeo clown and chiropractor. Adventure finally led him and his family to South Africa. The children's education was primarily aimed at teaching them self-sufficiency. With no punishments. Joshua assumed they would instinctively exhibit the correct behaviour. Elon's mother more or less applied the same educational tactic, albeit it not quite as extravagantly. She, too, gave her children plenty of room to make their own choices. And so, at eight years old, Elon chose to live with his father and was not impeded in the slightest when leaving for Canada at age 17.

Self-confidence: daring to take risks

Autonomy isn't just at the core of Elon Musk's every cell, he also possesses a fair amount of self-confidence. His faith in his own abilities and knowledge is massive. His encyclopedic knowledge and photographic memory is what he bases that faith on. Even without notes, he can still reproduce every single detail from a conversation or meeting that took place weeks ago. Things he can't remember, but does find important, he masters in record time. What doesn't interest him gets left by the wayside. His high degree of self-confidence makes him a no-holds-barred go-getter, who doesn't shy away from taking big risks. Mind you, those risks are always well-thought-out. Musk never sets out his course based solely on his intuition.

A born optimist: possibility within every difficulty

Musk is also a born optimist. He gushes with enthusiasm when it comes to realising his goals. His intrinsic motivation is that of the true 'yes man'. Every difficulty presents a possibility to

---

'Musk never sets out his course

based solely on his intuition.'

---

him. He doesn't think in problems, but in solutions. Mistakes are not a source of guilt or shame, but a possibility to learn that much faster. Don't, however, think Musk is naive or simply operates on blind optimism. No way! He's realistic enough to know what he's getting into and what the risks are. He simply utilises the positive energy that comes with optimism to its fullest extent.

Hope bringers sway you

Let's say you have the most creative and innovating idea in the world—if you can't convince others of that idea, you'll go home empty-handed, hope bringer or not. Musk knows the importance of shining a spotlight on his message of hope. He tries to fascinate his (potential) followers in every possible fashion. How? First of all, by going back to his fundamental premise every time: life on Earth is in danger and we need to be on the lookout for a back-up somewhere else in space. Next, he draws people in with a continuous flow of innovations that directly connect with that basic premise. Finally, he shares that message in a highly appealing way. Musk is capable of turning rocket launches, a quite dull thing nowadays, into a whole event. A live video stream (SpaceX Webcast) allows everyone to follow the launch. As a viewer, you are told exactly what to expect, down to the very second, and why it's so exciting and awesome. Even the chances of succeeding are told in advance: during the May 2016 launch it was 72 per cent (not just a rough two-thirds chance, but exactly 72 per cent). The commentators make the event sound like a thrilling match, with this question as the stakes: will this attempt succeed in breaking boundaries or will it fail?

The downside

You may have gotten the idea that Musk is some sort of saint, who only tells the most fabulous stories and has no dark side at all. Don't forget that Musk is only human, just like the rest of us, and has to deal with two forces that often hinder him. The first is exaggeration. Exaggerated autonomy often turns to willfulness and sometimes coercive behaviour. Exaggerated self-confidence leads to arrogance and exaggerated enthusiasm to unscrupulous passion. As will become clear in the following chapters, Musk sometimes struggles with balancing his darker side, not to carry on too far with his exaggerations.

Another thing that from time to time also hinders him, is his childhood. As a boy, Musk tried to avoid the tough South-African macho culture. He largely succeeded. And yet, he seems to have unconsciously adopted some important elements of that toughness.

His toughness towards hostile competitors and his low esteem of them is something we can understand. Business men are often street fighters, so don't act surprised when he says he considers Apple Tesla's graveyard, as Apple only snatches up Tesla's 'rotten apples'. His fierceness and toughness when making business decisions can also be justified—certainly at the level he competes at, where corporate management is simply not for the weak-minded. But even his most loyal employees can count on little sympathy.

When his follower and assistant of many years, Mary Beth Brown, asked for a raise, Musk told her off with the suggestion to take a few weeks' holiday. During that time, he would personally take on her tasks, to see how essential they were. Back from her holiday, she was handed her notice. If you want to save humankind, you don't start moaning about money. Another employee missed an event due to the birth of his child. Musk sent him the following e-mail in return: 'That is no excuse. I am extremely disappointed. You need to figure out where your priorities are. We're changing the world and changing history, and you either commit or you don't.'

Musk himself denies this latter incident, but there are plenty of tales from his employees and even his first ex-wife that demonstrate Musk regularly prefers the tough and negative approach to the soft and positive one. The goal justifies the means. Whoever wants to offer hope, must sometimes drive people to despair.

As Musk's biographer, Ashlee Vance, describes it: 'Musk's demanding management style can only flourish because of the otherworldly aspirations of the company.'

MUSK MINI MASTERCLASS:

HOPE BEGINS WITH TAKING YOUR OWN IDEA SERIOUSLY

You now know what makes Musk hope and how he then conveys it. Time to apply these lessons yourself:

- What is an important idea to you, which almost no one around you shares? Why is that one idea so important to you and why does it excite you? What problems will you fix with it?

- Try to not just formulate your idea in an inspiring way, but to also corroborate it with facts as much as you can.

- Continually make sure you're still 100 per cent behind the idea. Do you have enough self-confidence to promote the idea in the future? Do you really think you can use it to make a difference?

One more tip: the idea doesn't immediately need to involve saving humankind. You can leave that to Musk.

5

Principle 2:
Be aware of all things

'Just start with your idea, but keep asking
yourself what's going right and what isn't and
make sure you adjust to reality quickly.'

Elon Musk

**Aside from being a first-class hope bringer with wild ideas,
Musk is also an incredible observer. This is a second, crucial
quality of Wavemakers. Incredibly good observers are alert
and curious. They assume nothing, are open to new insights
and ask a thousand-and-one questions—with the undisputed
top three being: Why? Why not? What if? It allows them to
see things that others don't.**

What makes you an incredibly good observer? For starters,
you have to be able to look at reality in different ways, wide-
eyed and adventurous. You're attentive to what's happening
around you. You're curious and open to new insights. You
can take a step back and see the bigger picture, but also
focus on the smallest of details. Another thing that's typical
for an incredibly good observer: by looking at matters from
different perspectives, you avoid prejudiced viewpoints.

Incredibly good observers aren't just curious, but also capable of in-depth and systematic analyses. They want to know why things are the way they seem them. That way, they discover underlying connections and patterns, using logical analysis to merge their observations into a coherent vision. And that vision allows the incredibly good observer to focus on the things that matter to them.

A born doubter

However well you look at things and think them through, there's always the possibility that your image of reality is not completely accurate. Aside from that adventurous outlook and those in-depth analyses, the incredibly good observer also sets himself apart by way of a third quality: he never takes any conclusion at face value. Because the incredibly good observer is also a born doubter, one who's extremely critical when it comes to his own conclusions. An incredibly good observer therefore tries to undermine his own ideas in every way possible. And only when that doesn't work, does he consider a job well done.

Elon Musk is an incredibly good observer in every possible way. Alert and curious, he's capable of continuous shifts in perspective. He's a master of penetrating situation and event analyses. He steers his own, intransigent course. And he never lets up on his endless quest for critical facts to counter his own and other people's way of thinking.

The brain of the incredibly good observer

To understand how it works, we'll take a quick dive into the way the brain works and that of Musk in particular. Our brain is comprised of at least two parts: a primary system that works extremely fast and supplies us continuously with information and viewpoints on what we're observing. This allows us to make fast decisions based on little information. Let's say you're in the jungle and something is stirring in the bushes next to you. Your fast brain system rapidly warns you of a possible threat, say, a poisonous snake or a dangerous predator. This system is therefore sometimes called the 'flash brain'. Convenient when there's danger or, living in our hectic day and age, you have to make choices quickly.

Downside: the flash brain's quick presumptions are often highly inaccurate. Take this simple test by psychologist Daniel Kahneman. A bat and a ball together cost 1 euro and 10 cents. The bat is 1 euro more expensive than the ball. How expensive is the ball? A majority of people blurt out: 10 cents. And quick and easy answer from the flash brain, without really thinking about it. If you do, you'll know that that answer can't be right. A bat that's 1 euro more expensive than the ball and a ball costing 10 cents, make a total of 1 euro and 20 cents. The correct answer isn't 10 cents, but 5 cents. You can figure this out by questioning your first, intuitive answer and then getting to work with your second brain system: the slower and logical part.

Musk makes good use of his second, slower and rational brain system. Our first brain system isn't just focused on eliminating danger, but also entices us to keep thinking that which we've always been thinking. This is how, in the 19th century, the quest for improvements in transport resulted in breeding stronger horses. A new mode of transport didn't occur to the quick flash brains. That took a wholly different and more rational way of thinking, one that didn't take the familiar world of horses and carriages as a jumping board, but asked a far more fundamental question: what are the basic conditions for forward motion? Only the person who asks that question can think of the idea of a steam or combustion engine. Still horse power—just a different kind. This is exactly the kind of question Musk poses.

Iconoclasts

Let's quickly summarize: incredibly good observers dare to question existing realities, see things others do not, are prepared to experiment, have the courage to make mistakes and coalesce widely differing fragments of knowledge and information into a new and logical whole. Neuroscientist Gregory Berns calls these people iconoclasts. People who attack and topple conventional ideas. 'To see things differently than other people, the most effective solution is to bombard the brain with things it has never encountered before,' Berns writes with regards to iconoclasts. 'Novelty releases the perceptual process from the shackles of past experience and forces the brain to make new judgments.'

Clearly, Elon Musk is one of these iconoclasts. Musk himself called this way of 'deep thinking' a quest for the First Principle: dissect everything you see and value into logical parts, take nothing for granted, ask as many critical questions as you can think of and try to come to truths in a logical and systematic way, so that you can base new insights on these truths. Don't try to let quick, but often incorrect, suppositions from the primary brain system lead you. Instead, try using your second, rational brain system to find new chances and possibilities. Such as developing a much cheaper and more powerful battery, an electric car or a rocket headed for Mars.

Negative feedback please

To discover the First Principles, you require a systematic mind and a large degree of concentration. Above all, however, you need to be permanently receptive to criticism. Musk demands continuous negative feedback on all his wild and hopeful ideas. He disdains yes-men and ass-kissers. Dissenting Musk thereby challenges the accepted notion that others are best motivated by positive encouragement. Compliments are good for the ego, but bad for the quality of your products, he says. Only a (self-)critical attitude helps you grow. And this is what he tries to stimulate as much he can. 'I always immediately ask people what they don't like about it. If I ask people to test a product, I always only want them to tell me what they think is wrong with it. Tell me the bad news straight away and to the point. Spend only a

---

'Musk demands continuous negative feedback

on all his wild and hopeful ideas.'

---

little of my time on good news, focus on the bad. I always spend more time on the bad news than on the good news,' he says. The negative feedback keeps him sharp and alert. False hope is something that doesn't occur for him. That (self-)critical attitude is something he also demands from his team. 'Nobody is perfect, everybody makes mistakes. I want my people to come to me directly if they're working on something they expect to go wrong. If I know about it in time, I can react. Sometimes, people think they can fix something before it gets out of hand. Maybe they can, but I still want to know about it. Everyone makes mistakes. But someone who doesn't report a mistake to me, lets a problem occur, thinks he can solve it himself and then still lets it get out of control, can almost certainly count on getting fired.'

Musk wants to first understand and explain everything, as well as making sure it all has a basis in science, before commencing on anything. He quickly penetrates to the core of any issue, easily tracks down unseen patterns and spots unexpected connections. He doesn't stay mired in vague dreams, but makes everything concrete by zooming in and out. Experimentation brings him to new insights. But once a certain vision has nestled in his mind, nothing and no one can dislodge it. However long it may take.

MUSK MINI MASTERCLASS:

STAY ALERT AND CRITICAL

As an incredibly good observer, Musk sees potential where others do not. He does this by zooming in and out, continually asking critical questions and basing the answers to those questions in science. How can you yourself apply this lesson?

- Be no less curious than Musk and try to get a bird's eye view of the reality around you. What is the bigger picture you see? Next, zoom in on the details. Which of these draws your eye?

- While doing so, keep asking critical questions: why do things happen the way they do? Why isn't it done differently? What would happen if...?

- Do like Musk and try to penetrate the fundamental essence of the subject you find most important. Go back to the basis of corroborated facts and hypotheses. Use these as a jumping-off point to try and logically reason backwards until you've found the best solution.

A tip for the latter: Take an empty sheet of paper and make two columns. In the left column, write what you know for sure. In the right column, write what you get stuck on. Look closely at what point and when the latter happens and try to come to the most logical solution.

6

Principle 3:
Aim for Mars

'The first step is to establish that something is

possible; then probability will occur.'

Elon Musk

Think big. That is the third principle of the Wavemaker. It certainly applies to Elon Musk. Big, bigger, biggest: rummaging along the wayside is not for him. He thrives on visionary vistas and boundless ambitions. At the same time, Musk demonstrates himself to be a master when it comes to strategic flexibility. He therein quite resembles a simultaneous chess player, who plays on several chessboards at the same time and moves pawns in an equally thought-out and surprising manner.

In the entire history of the human race, it's never been so easy to realise great things. Technology enables us to better communicate with each other, information and knowledge is at everyone's fingertips and we're more productive and healthier than ever. At the same time, technologies make it more difficult than ever for us to realise what we truly find important. The communicative twittering and the urge for ever-increasing productivity surrounding us creates a lot of noise, to the point where it's become nearly impossible to distinguish the signals that are important to us. The incoming stream of data makes that our attention is continually divided and we find it increasingly difficult to focus on important tasks.

Our lives are therefore often dominated by trivial to-do's: plans and tasks we feel obligated to realise as soon as we can. We increase the pressure even further by wanting to realize several of these trivial goals simultaneously. Our focus on a thousand-and-one things makes us no longer reflect on matters. The pressure has become so great that we mostly look only at what's right in front of us, instead of focusing on the bigger and, more often than not, future goals. The unintended side effect of all our fussing around: we lose track of what's truly important and what we really want. We make ourselves smaller than we are. And we leave a huge amount of potential unused.

An incredibly important dream

How do you break through this cycle? Focus on one or several incredibly important dreams for a longer period of time, dreams you want to achieve no matter the cost. A tried method that even President John F. Kennedy utilised. In the 1960s, the Americans, to their shame, had to admit they had lost their technological lead in space travel on the Russians. The reason: NASA was chasing after no less than 531 goals at the same time. Departments were working against instead of with each other. Most employees were completely in the dark as to what NASA stood for, let alone what it was aiming for. To turn the tide, Kennedy decided to take a step that was as unusual as it was effective: he cancelled all those goals and replaced them with a dream. The dream of having a man on the moon within 10 years and having them come home safely. He mentioned in multiple speeches that it wasn't just a dream, but an incredibly important dream—one deeply rooted in the American values of showing guts and breaking boundaries. NASA rediscovered its focus and was able to realize seemingly impossible technological breakthroughs within a minimal amount of time. The dream turned out to be contagious: when the first astronauts set foot on the moon, a true 'Moon Mania' erupted all over the country and throughout large parts of the world.

'Kennedy cancelled all those 531 goals

and replaced them with a dream.'

Moon shots: ten times better

The focus on realising incredibly important dreams dwindled into the background after that. Until American high-tech corporations rediscovered it this century. Google especially has been industriously working away at its so-called 'moon shots': highly ambitious and important projects with a big risk profile and little chance of success. The level of ambition is usually expressed with the formula '10x'. These projects should produce products and services that are ten times better than any now existing. The idea behind it is that it's often easier to make something ten times better than ten per cent better. Someone wanting to make things ten per cent better takes what's already extant and, by working harder and acquiring more means, thinks he can make his way one step at a time. To make things ten times better, you shouldn't be moved by convention, but by what you require. For this purpose, a somewhat secretive innovation centre has been created: Google X. Google's founders and owners have given this center the authorisation to think big. With success: Google X is currently thinking up self-driving cars, ways to combat cancer and Wi-Fi balloons that will float in the stratosphere. These plans do fail from time to time, as was evident with the first version of the Google Glass.

Mars shots

You can even take it one step further. Musk doesn't aim for the moon, but for Mars. An ambition rooted in Musk's life philosophy that life on Earth has become so vulnerable that someday we'll be forced to relocate to other planets. Musk's goal is for the first rockets to be sent to Mars in 2018 and the first people in 2030. Round about the middle of the century there should be roughly one million people living on the red planet. They'll start the creation of an extraterrestrial civilization, while simultaneously forming a 'back-up' population, should things here on Earth go completely downhill.

Were Elon Musk only an amazing dreamer and hope bringer, this would've been the end of it.

But to a thinker and strategist this vision by itself is insufficient. He wants to figure out exactly how to reach that goal. Naturally, Musk realises that building up a rocket venture or car company from scratch is an impossible task. After all, you're up against very powerful and influential opponents. At the same time, he sees plenty of opportunity for companies that, with a clean slate, start operating in industrial sectors that have barely developed over the course of the last half-century with regards to innovation. Musk largely bypasses those existing companies and focuses on new and unexploited market sectors. The literature on strategy calls this the 'blue ocean' approach: you go out on uncharted waters. It takes guts and business know-how, but at least you prevent your immediately being crushed by strong competitors, who wish to defend their market in any way possible, both savory and less savoury.

Despite the fact that he holds to his eventual ambition of going to Mars, he continually chooses different strategic routes to get there. Just as with Rome, all roads lead to Mars.

SpaceX's low-cost strategy

What do you do when you want to enter a market dominated by parties like Boeing and Lockheed? Companies that experience so little competition they've become arrogant, and who mostly offer top-of-the-line products for exorbitant prices? To Musk, what they're doing is along the lines of building a Ferrari while a perfectly good mid-range car can easily equal their performance. Musk sees a golden opportunity here: he's not committed to offering the best of the best, but to producing relatively cheap and reusable rockets on the market's lower segments. This low-cost strategy has turned to be a stroke of genius, which serves at least a three-fold purpose. Firstly, by focusing on a completely new market segment, Musk avoids directly confronting his current and powerful competitors. Secondly, Musk's strategy is garnering him immediate streams of revenue, which he needs to maintain his company and finance further space adventures. After all, with his low-cost strategy, Musk is meeting the growing demand for the provisioning of space stations and launching small satellites. He's not only managed to secure those funds by way of a lucrative cooperation with NASA, it also prevents the danger of empty coffers after the three previous failed rocket launches. The company is sitting ever more comfortably, partly due to SpaceX's probable future production and launching of its own satellites.

Eventually, however, it's of course all about the trip to Mars. The incoming revenue is used by SpaceX to realise that goal. Musk is also continually thinking in terms of win-win: it's not just his current business partners who profit from an expected 99 per cent reduction in costs, but travels to Mars also benefit from affordable and reusable rockets. While a ticket to Mars is a mere ten billion dollars per person in 2016, it's Musk's aim to have it come down to 500,000 dollars. That's 20,000 times less. Musk also kills several birds with one stone. For example, a world-encompassing system of satellites doesn't just provide a continuous cash flow and internet connections in every corner of the globe, but also provides the basis for a communications platform in space.

Sometimes it seems as if Musk is just randomly doing stuff. Even his own staff sometimes think so. To avoid a lot of questions in people, Musk regularly dons his writing cap to elucidate. He then never fails to point out the importance of the fundamental goal: making life on Mars possible.

Tesla: start small before outdoing others

Just as with his space adventures, Musk had a clear vision from the start of what he wanted a car company to do: not offering stocks or selling cars to just a chosen few rich people. No, the eventual goal is overturning the current automobile industry. Cars should develop from gas-guzzling monsters based on outdated technology into quiet and beautifully-designed vehicles that make you look cool.

When starting his own car brand, Musk utilized the by now well-known principle of incredibly good entrepreneurship: he travelled throughout the country to exchange thoughts with all kinds of electric car inventors. Eventually, he partnered up with two men who started a small company for the development of electric luxury cars: Tesla Motors. The name is an homage to Nikola Tesla, a famed and idealistic inventor and electricity expert.

The capitalistic automobile market may not appear to have any room for newcomers. But, just as with the development of his aerospace plans, he sees a world in motion and a market that is most certainly interested in electric cars. To turn it into a success, you simply have to be an uncompromising innovator. Not by innovating because your regulators tell you to, as existing car brands do, but because you truly want to.

Where Musk was able to avoid the competition of existing aerospace companies by focusing on the as-yet untapped market of affordable and reusable rockets, he chose a different strategic path for Tesla: make yourself small before trying to outdo others. Musk started developing an attractive sports car, the Roadster, aimed at the not very important profit-wise but eye-catching luxury market segment. Clever, as you won't immediately upset the competition by starting off in such a relatively small segment. Furthermore, he can use wealthy celebrities to draw people's attention. Another plus: as the new guy on the market, he can begin working on developing his electric car mostly undisturbed.

Strategical openness

On the other hand, undisturbed? The remarkable thing about Musk is that he publishes his strategic intentions quite early on. In a masterplan he published in 2006, he lets people know he intends to market the sports car (Roadster) first. With the money he earns he wants to start making a saloon (Model S) for a broader, but still quite well-off target group. Only after that will there be an affordable electric car (Model 3) for the general public put out on the market.

Strategical documents and masterplans are generally tiresome papers which are developed in private and kept secret. Not so with Elon Musk, as became clear when he presented his ten-year horizon in the midst of 2016. He turned this into a carefully orchestrated media event, the new developments where announced with the same audacity as a blockbuster movie. Both the competition and his followers where eagerly awaiting the event. The date was postponed several times because the main character couldn't find the time to wrap things up, with his schedule filled with things like a rocket launch (and successful landing) and the grand opening of his gigantic battery factory (Gigafactory). But suddenly it was on the company website: 'the Tesla Masterplan, Part Deux'. Its publication created a media explosion, it was the main topic of conversation that day. Thousands of bloggers shared their views, expert opinions were tumbling all over each other. But everyone agreed on one thing. Though it sometimes appears from the outside that Musk is just fooling around, he does use these clear strategic frames to his advantage. And not only that, he is so self-assured that he will tell everyone

Elon Musk, the mastermind
behind Tesla and SpaceX.

In January 2018, SpaceX published this photo of the Falcon Heavy Demo Mission on launch pad 39A of the Kennedy Space Center. The Falcon Heavy is currently the most powerful rocket in the world, and according to SpaceX at least twice as powerful as its competition.

April 8th 2016, an important moment in the journey towards recyclable rockets: the successful landing of a Falcon-9 missile on the drone ship Of Course I Still Love You.

▲
▲ A historical moment in 2012, the delivery of the first Tesla Model S by Tesla CTO J.B. Straubel (right).

▲ Always searching for improvement, Tesla uses robots.

▶ Musk in his element at Tesla's annual shareholders meeting, photographed by an acquaintance.

◀ Every advantage has its disadvantage: rockets that are able to land require storage space.

Musk expects to land people on Mars in 2024.

The Hyperloop is a concept for an innovative means of transportation.
Elon Musk's role is limited to inspiratory, for the time being.

exactly what he's up to. There will be a lot more versions of the popular Tesla cars, a pickup truck is in the making and the first electric Tesla truck was presented by the end of 2017.

Tesla: from car factory to energy company

The new masterplan also announced the transformation that has been realised. It is no longer a car factory (Tesla Motors) but a full-fledged energy company (Tesla). It was the formalisation of a development that had started a few years ago. When it became apparent that the current battery factories couldn't meet Tesla's high demands, Elon Musk decided to take matters into his own hands. A team of top engineers tinkered until they had a battery that excelled in both performance and safety. To guarantee its availability, a futuristic factory was built in the midst of the Nevada desert: the Gigafactory. It should produce over half a million batteries by 2020.

It's a small step from batteries to solar energy. It's another subject Musk studied in depth while at college, but wasn't able to get around to due to lack of time. Until two of his cousins, with whom he grew up in South Africa and who have since also emigrated to the United States, ask him if he can think of a new challenge for the pair. Something that earns them good money and makes them feel good. Musk directs them towards solar energy. After a thorough investigation of the market, they founded SolarCity in 2006. The ultimate goal: making solar panels possible and affordable for regular consumers by way of an all-inclusive service strategy. There's a few obstacles to get by: the costs of solar panels are high and installing them is often problematic. The men realise financial provision by offering software indicating whether or not solar energy is cost-effective and the option of leasing solar panels. With their own teams to install solar panels,

SolarCity quickly becomes the largest installer in the United States.

SolarCity goes public in 2012, already worth seven billion dollars by that time. A side note here is that more than two-thirds of that amount have evaporated. What everyone feared—especially in the United States—became reality, currently sustainable energy is still an impossible market. It was a logical, but not undisputed, decision to incorporate the loss-making company into the parent company. And so it happened. Tesla is gradually turning into a sustainable energy company. Which means that there is even more vigour for the new ideas, like fashionable solar roof tiles to replace the unsightly solar panels. And like all of that isn't enough, near Melbourne, Australia, they will soon start building a suburban town based upon all Elon Musk's ideas and visions. It will be eco-friendly and equipped with all the benefits of digital technology. It was named YarraBend, but the people nearby just call it Tesla Town.

Elon Musk's business imperium

Musk is on fire: he's bursting with energy to take off into space, and also to turn the world upside down as soon as he can. Goals that many had already more or less deemed write-offs, things like producing electric cars or relatively affordable and high-efficiency batteries, he breathes back into life. And he keeps on launching new ideas and ambitions, such as a super-fast way of transportation, electric airplanes that can take off and land horizontally and a world-encompassing network of satellites to make the internet accessible in every far-flung corner of the globe and space around us.

All of these ideas together have led to an ever-expanding

ecosystem of businesses that he runs or finances. The core of his empire is formed by Tesla and SpaceX. Around these two there has grown a colourful tangle of activity[2]. The nature of this activity and how it is controlled is adaptable to the circumstances. Like the Hyperloop, the ultrafast means of transportation that Musk once invented and which we shall discuss later on. Due to lack of time, he put the idea in other people's hands at first—inventors, entrepreneurs and idealists—but it appears he has changed his mind and wants to develop the idea himself now.

From some of his ideas the status is unclear. We can only guess whether there is top-secret activity put into the development of electronic airplanes (that can also take-off and land vertically). And nothing is certain about the status of the earlier announced global network of satellites to enable internet access in all the far corners of space. But don't be surprised when Musk whips up another revolutionary idea. Which happened when he coolly announced a new start-up in the Spring of 2017, the Boring Company. It wasn't a joke, it really is a company that is capable of drilling tunnels at lightning speed. This would not only boost Musk's hyperfast means of transportation (Hyperloop), but it could also end traffic jams in metropolitan areas. At the first presentation

---

2   Musk is on fire: he's bursting with energy to take off into space, and also to turn the world upside down as soon as he can. Goals that many had already more or less deemed write-offs, things like producing electric cars or relatively affordable and high-efficiency batteries, he breathes back into life. And he keeps on launching new ideas and ambitions, such as a super-fast way of transportation, electric airplanes that can take off and land horizontally and a world-encompassing network of satellites to make the internet accessible in every far-flung corner of the globe and space around us.

this Spring, we saw a science-fiction video[3], in which cars drove through elevators off the road into the tunnels to be absorbed by traffic flow. How he got this idea? He used logical thinking. 'Nowadays machines use half the time to dig tunnels and half the time to reinforce the tunnels they just dug,' he said like he had years of experience in this field. 'I want to develop a machine that does this simultaneously.' And he quickly added that he had already started drilling a tunnel through Los Angeles. One of the entrances just happens to be nearby his L.A.-based SpaceX offices. Typical Elon Musk...

---

3   See the video on the YouTube channel from The Boring Company:

www.youtube.com/watch?v=5V_VzRrSBI

MUSK MINI MASTERCLASS:

DARE TO CHASE YOUR BIGGEST AMBITIONS

Crossing boundaries and realising breakthrough achievements starts by formulating exciting, inspiring and challenging ambitions, as Musk demonstrates. It's also equally important to be flexible in the manner in which you realise those ambitions. How can you apply this yourself?

- Think: what's your biggest ambition? Which problem would you like to fix? Does the solution you have in mind make things ten times (or more!) better? Does it truly energise you and are you willing to chase after your ambition without compromise?

- Take a strategic take on determining your path(s): how will you go about realising your ambition? Did you think carefully on why you chose or didn't choose a certain strategy? Are you sure this is the right way to success?

- Let's say you're on your way and your initial strategy is turning out to not be that good after all. What will you do? Do you let it defeat you into giving up your ambition? Do you tenaciously press on with your original strategy? Or do you demonstrate strategic flexibility and simply choose a different path?

7

Principle 4:
Play to win

How does Musk manage to keep all those balls in the air? It might be because he sees his work as a game. Musk is as super fanatical and extremely motivated as a gamer. He gets in a flow every day, stopping at nothing to achieve his goals. Losing does not feature in his vocabulary. That, too, is a quality of a true Wavemaker: never giving up and being in it to win it.

It's a Saturday when Ashlee Vance, busy on writing Musk's biography, visits him at Tesla's Palo Alto headquarters. It was the weekend, but the parking lot was packed full of cars. Hundreds of people were hard at work in the building. He tells Musk he's impressed with this remarkable work ethic. Musk didn't agree and began complaining about the fact that increasingly less people were coming in to work during the weekends: 'We're becoming a damn bunch of softies.'

One of SpaceX's first employees—designated by his number on the list: #23—had previously worked for one of its competitors. There, he had become used to a lot of

---

'I was dead on my feet and

mentally off-kilter, but I soon grew to

love it and became totally addicted.'

---

talking and discussing, but not much action. SpaceX was the complete opposite. After he got the job, he was told he had to take care of his own office supplies. After that, it was fasten your seatbelt and he was up to his eyebrows in work. He was making 12-hour days, sleeping for ten hours and then coming straight back to the factory. 'I was dead on my feet and mentally off-kilter,' he says in Ashlee Vance's biography, 'but I soon grew to love it and became totally addicted.'

Bringing your sleeping bag to work

The secret behind his remarkable successes really sounds very old-fashioned: hard work. Musk chooses a goal he truly believes in and then goes off full steam ahead, day and night, until that goal has been reached. He's not distracted by trivial matters, but challenges others to just give that little extra and outdo their own expectations.

Whoever works for or with Musk find themselves in a kind of boot camp, where you get pushed to your limit and don't get a moment's peace. Twelve-hour work days and six-day work weeks are the standard. And a lot of employees work even longer. Working for Musk means you get sent on impossible missions. You have to fulfill them by your own wits. And in the meantime, you get harangued with new demands or earlier deadlines. And you know that during all this, the boss's eyes are constantly on you. There's a reason why Elon Musk has his desk in the middle of the working area. It makes him easy to reach, but it also enables him to keep an eye on everything. Day and night, if possible. Literally.

And so, in May 2016, Musk announces that Tesla has revised its ambitions and wants to produce no less than 500,000 cars by 2018. Originally, this was the goal for 2020. And that was already something critics were doubtful of, considering the record number in 2015 was a 'mere' 50,000. But Musk advances the deadline by another two years. At the same time, he doubles the goal for 2020 to one million cars. Two of his top managers choose that moment to quit. A few days later, and Musk has almost completed his team again: he's lured away a production star from a German competitor. Those deadlines, by the way, are not a goal to him, but a means to improve the world with his inventions as soon as possible: 'Of course we're not going to make those 500,000 cars by 2018. And those one million cars in 2020 are going to be nothing short of a challenge. But we'll do our best and I've got a sleeping bag in a room adjacent to the floor.'

Dedication bordering addiction

Can't keep up the pace? Then you can take an extra-long vacation. There will be no need to come back. Working for Musk means dedication bordering addiction—in a time where jobs elsewhere are mostly about 'doing what you like'. Sweet dreams, or so Musk would say. Those who work hard and work with dedication, will go further and achieve more. That's how it was and how it still is.

His own commitment knows no limits. A typical work week sees him start with a day and a half at the SpaceX factory in Los Angeles, then travelling by private jet to one of the offices and factories of Tesla, to then return to SpaceX at the end of the week. In between, he also busies himself with the other companies of his ecosystem, together with thinking of and announcing new technological and business innovations, networking with managers and politicians, negotiations for new production facilities, attending rocket launches and giving presentations. He also has five sons. They mostly get his time and attention during weekends.

Uncontained energy

Friends and foes agree on one thing: Musk abounds with energy. According to his ex-wife Justine, his body is like a tank. 'His stamina and resilience towards stress are unequalled.' He's used to working non-stop and completely shutting the world out if necessary. Musk demonstrates enormous resilience: the ability to focus on one or several tasks, without losing your attention to other matters, such as incoming e-mails, apps and meetings.

Where does Musk get the energy from? It's partially a surplus of energy he was simply born with, but his energy also feeds from several sources. Like the focus on goals and activities he truly believes in. His passion doesn't come from the need for wealth or fame. Musk follows his calling. He does things because he wants to and believes in them.

A second source of energy is his curiosity and inquisitiveness. Each new thought and every new initiative provide him with more energy than he's expending.

The third energy source is his achievements. It's really very simple: achievements energise you. Every athlete knows this.

A lot of managers have unfortunately forgotten. They usually achieve as expected, which normally leaves you achieving average results. And mediocrity rarely gives you energy. Not surprising then that Musk fights against mediocrity.

Alexander the Geat

His ambitions are insatiable. The work is never done and there's always the possibility of smarter, faster and better. Alexander the Great is an example to him for a reason. He, too, was a strategic innovator, empire builder and with an insatiable appetite. Alexander had one goal in mind: getting to the Endless Ocean, where the Greeks thought the known world ended. To achieve it, he and his army penetrated deep into the Indian continent. At every river or mountain range blocking their path, he encouraged his men by saying it was just a matter of grinding your teeth and going on. After all, they were almost there.

Musk may not be a world conqueror in the literal meaning of the word, but his passion and perseverance are no less than Alexander's. He's prepared to risk everything. He continuously pushes his employees to perform better and regularly drives them to despair. And any possible obstacles such as laws or practical issues? Those are swept unceremoniously aside. Musk only examines the way in which he can realise his wishes. One example: in order to realise a fast fibreglass connection between his offices, he required the right of way from his neighbors. When they refused, he and his manager came up with a ruse. The fibreglass cables were hidden inside regular, aboveground electricity and telephone cables. 'We did that in one weekend, instead of having to wait months for permits,' the manager said.

Nano-manager

That rebellious side also has its opposite. Musk can also behave like a controlling and intimidating micro-manager towards his usually very loyal staff. Musk proudly calls himself a nano-manager. He wants to be involved in every detail. The tiniest of grammatical errors in e-mails are immediately punished and in case of even the smallest of imperfections in products he has the entire production process halted. Everything has to be perfect. And it's only perfect when Musk says it is. Don't come to him with half-assed excuses or explanations that you did things the way you did because that's the way it's always done. You will without doubt get chided at, with a cannonade of swearing thrown your way for good measure.

The rush of the game

Aside from the fact that they're enthused by Musk's mission, there's another factor why Musk and his employees are willing to make extremely long work days: they turn their work into a game until they enter a flow. Just like a video game. Those games do seem to run like a red thread through Musk's life and work. He marketed his first video game when he was 12. He's also a highly fanatical player. A few years ago, when an American journalist visited Musk for a series of interviews, she found him in the basement, focused on a video game. The room was designed for it, with a couch, an enormous television screen and a table for the game console. The gigantic basement was otherwise empty.

That minimalistic decoration also applies to the rest of the house. Despite having five children, there's no kids' stuff. Nothing points to the presence of pets, even though he has two dogs. No single shred of evidence pointing to a female presence, despite Musk still being officially married during that time. Personal elements, such as photographs or travel mementoes, are equally lacking. Musk clearly likes a fresh and clean appearance. You seem the same in his offices. The floors of the factories and offices of Tesla and SpaceX have a shining epoxy coating and the walls are a stainless white. That's right: like a giant gaming space.

Overcoming obstacles

Gaming then seems not just a metaphor, but also a shining example of his work method. Games are distinguished by the fact of there being a clear end goal. To achieve that goal, you have to solve a slew of problems and overcome various obstacles. You're operating in a continuously changing environment. You have to constantly make decisions and undertake activities. Scores are closely kept. You therefore know exactly if you're making progress or not. Two further crucial hallmarks of a video game: you participate voluntarily and you're playing to win. From others, but also from yourself. Challenges and competition make a game exciting and keep you busy playing for hours, days and months.

Musk doesn't just play games at home. When travelling from one city to the other, he regularly stays over with friends. They often hear him cursing and swearing deep into the night, fighting virtual opponents and achieving noble quests. At work, when it's time for the evening break, everyone comes together to play fighting games that involve mowing down as many opponents as you can. Musk is a fanatical player even then and a regular winner, knowing all the tricks to get at his opponents. Because Musk is in it to win it. Literally and figuratively.

MUSK MINI MASTERCLASS:

TAKE RISKS AND TRY TO WIN

Musk plays to win. He doesn't just make long hours, but is also capable of focusing fully on his tasks. How can you apply this yourself?

- How big is your intrinsic motivation (you can also call it drive or passion) to win in the areas you find important? What do you really want to achieve? To what degree do you want rise above yourself to achieve things you've never achieved before?

- To what degree are you capable of not losing your attention when you're under pressure? Do you demonstrate sufficient willpower to achieve your goal, no matter the cost? Or do you quit easily? If so, why and to what degree can you change this?

Tip: don't let the story of having to multitask like Musk mislead you. Because that's not what Musk's doing. What he is doing: continuously finishing one task in his mind and then directly going on to the next one. That is something quite different: serial single-tasking.

8

Principle 5:
Move people

'If you wake up in the morning

and think the future is going to be better,

it is a bright day. Otherwise, it's not.'

Elon Musk

Without a doubt, Musk is master when it comes to inspiring people. He's clever and has a continuously contrary and scientific mindset. He chases after the greatest of ambitions and likes to hold the reins while doing so. He's passionate through and through. But a master of emotional and social aspects? That is perhaps a touch more difficult to imagine. And yet, like no other, he has a way of gathering people to him. He does so purposely: he knows you can't make waves alone—that always requires others. This is the fifth principle of Wavemakers.

The image we created of Musk in the previous chapters is that of a genius prodigy and heroic leader. This places us safely within the confines of the long and impressive tradition of publications on 'extraordinary men'. It's the hallmark of this tradition to laud the individual qualities and achievements of loners. This generally creates a rather one-sided and incomplete picture. Also, you can never credit achievements 100 per cent to one individual. To some degree, achievements always depend on the input and support of others. Even Alexander the Great, Elon Musk's role model, was in the end dependent on his men's support and willingness to fight. When his soldiers, tired and exhausted from all the deprivations, refused to continue marching to the Endless Ocean, even this world conqueror had no other choice than to head back.

Positive emotions, please

Musk is generally considered to be a super smart nerd, who mostly deals in rational brain power and does not possess a great deal of emotional and social brain power. Indeed, based on what his family members, ex-wives and (former) employees say about him, he's not really all that adept at regulating and vocalising his emotions. Negative emotions, such as the loss of his firstborn to SIDS, are best avoided as far as he's concerned: 'I'm not sure why I'd want to talk about extremely sad events. It does no good for the future. I'm not sure what should be done in such situations.' He's more comfortable expressing positive emotions. But even that he prefers doing around people he works with closely and whom he knows intimately. His attitude during public events is usually distant and hesitating. He clearly doesn't know how to respond to all those praises. And because he doesn't know exactly what to tell such an extensive and hopeful-minded audience, the words can sometimes be garbled with mutterings and stuttering. Add to this his notoriety in being brutally tough when breaking off personal and business relations ('you'd do well not to go to war with him'), his occasional crankiness and regular angry outbursts, and the picture that's painted is not exactly one of an emotionally stable and socially adept leader.

With thanks, humanity

When you look at Musk's personality profile, his lack of empathy and social skills is not all that surprising. That's just the nature of the beast. Empathy is an abstract term to Musk, which he's more inclined to project onto humanity as a whole than on individuals. This causes him to sometimes completely ignore his own or other people's feelings, but also to become very emotional when the subject is something as abstract as humanity. His fans know and appreciate this. When Musk was with his brother in a fast food restaurant, an unknown person bought them a drink with a note attached, thanking them for 'a future that inspires us to be a part of it'. Signed: humanity.

Thanks to his crazy smart brain and desire to always learn new things, Musk manages to compensate his emotional and social shortcomings where it matters. What he doesn't feel spontaneously, he's purposely mastered. In effect, this actually makes him emotionally and socially 'smart'. You can see it in the way he socialises. His social sense is naturally focused on things that interest him intellectually or things he wants to realise no matter the cost. Musk, as a true Mastermind, is very selective in entering social relationships. And yet, he effortlessly moves between different social worlds. You can regularly find him in political or managerial circles to promote his business plans, but also taking to social media to share his new products. He shares his innovative ideas as open source, if it serves his corporate goals. And, if he doesn't have time, he's even inclined to let others take on the finalising of important ideas, like that superfast transport method. After all, it helps him realise his goals.

The staying power of a Superboss

This latter fact makes him an appealing leader to many people. One American study among graduates had almost a third (32 per cent) name Musk the most ideal mentor. The next person to come somewhat close was Bill Gates (23.8 per cent). Other well-known leaders, like Tim Cook of Apple, Google's Larry Page and Jeff Bezos of Amazon score less than 5 per cent each. The most prominent reasons of Musk's popularity as a leader: his eye for refreshing talent, giving people leeway to think of new things and then executing them as that person sees fit. That he calls them like he sees them is an added bonus. That honesty is appreciated by young people.

All in all, you can say Musk is a 'Superboss': a leader who's not just good at discovering talent, but also has an undeniably strong appeal to excellent achievers. However despicable their behaviour sometimes is, Superbosses have staying power. Based on a long-term study by American professor Sydney Finkelstein, Superbosses are normally known to be autonomous, very self-confident, dedicated one hundred per cent to their vision and exhibit a mixture of competitive and caring behavior.

Musk, too, is always on the lookout for new talent, people with the X factor—the X factor being: the drive and qualities to realise his mission. To further this goal, he doesn't just pay regular visits to universities, but also has a knack for spotting unknown talents. Take Tom Mueller. Mueller has been building small rockets ever since he was little. After graduating, he worked for major aerospace companies, where he was given free rein to experiment with new rocket engines. He hangs out with kindred spirits in his free time, some of whom quit their jobs to build rockets in their private workshops. Musk looks him up one Sunday in 2002, barraging Mueller with hundreds of questions. After meeting for hours, Musk is convinced and appoints Mueller a 'founding employee' of SpaceX. He's vice-president now.

Presenting challenges and creating maneuvering room

Even a Superboss can't be expected to personally recruit all 5,000 SpaceX and all 14,000 Tesla employees. There's standard procedures in place for that nowadays, which you'll also see other high-tech companies utilise. A potential candidate is subjected to a series of tests and interviews. Sometimes relaxed, but sometimes very intense. If you've successfully navigated that procedure, you have one task remaining: write an essay for Musk in which you explain your reasons for wanting to work for the company. In the early days, this was followed by a personal meeting with the big man himself. By now, this is granted only to the higher-placed employees. Once hired, you get your own office supplies and get to work as soon as possible. With an impossible assignment, of course. After all, that's the norm in Musk's companies.

Of course, Superbosses like Musk do much more than just recruiting and selecting talent. They create an open culture, wherein they provide people with the room to get moving themselves. They lead the vanguard and set the right example. And they also know when is a good time to say goodbye to one another. They constantly keep in mind the fact that talent stops growing at a certain point and wants to spread its wings. When that happens, the next generation of talent is already lining the block.

Drill instructor

Articles and books on new leadership often mention that the time of bosses is done. There's a trend of 'unbossing'. And even if there is a need for bosses, it's only for gentle and caring ones, who mostly dedicate themselves to inspiring, facilitating, empathising, coaching and communicating. A Superboss like Musk doesn't come anywhere close to this profile. He's more a mix of what Finkelstein describes iconoclasts to be—intractable and visionary leaders who mostly do their own thing—and glorious bastards, leaders who want to win regardless of the cost. Affection and likeability are not Musk's territory. Oftentimes, he mostly resembles a drill instructor.

If you work at SpaceX or Tesla, don't expect extensive thanks for a job well done. Chances are you'll get the question hurled at you why you couldn't have finished sooner. You should also be prepared for the newsflash that your work was all for nothing, as another direction has been chosen in the meantime. Too bad. On first meeting the big Boss, his assistant warns you upfront: 'Elon will likely keep on writing e-mails and working during the initial part of the interview and not speak much. Don't panic. That's normal. Eventually, he will turn around in his chair to face you.' You can also forget about endless and in-depth coaching talks. Musk is more likely to put you to an inquisition of sharp and confronting questions. Preferably answered correctly right off the bat.

The Musk working culture is one of few words and mostly doing. Everything has to be done quickly, quickly, quickly. Musk continuously harangues you to deliver a better performance. If there's a problem, there's Musk. Worktime isn't over until the problem is fixed. Usually with Musk leading the charge. Because despite it all, Musk is anything but an aloof leader who thinks up his plans somewhere high over the working place. He's at the centre of his predominantly male employees and clearly present. Occasionally, this sets the scene for some heartbreakingly tender moments of a group of guys working Sundays and talking tech shop at night while eating pizza. And, naturally, about winning tomorrow's battle...

'As a leader, Musk

is more commander-in-chief

than a CEO.'

Special units

Working for Musk is a life experience. Just like working in the Army's special units. SpaceX's website even mentions a comparison to the elite soldiers, the special forces: 'We have goals that are absurdly ambitious by any reasonable standard, but we're going to make them happen.' The reference to special forces is not present on Tesla's website —they mention 'a genuine passion for producing the best vehicles in the world' and 'These jobs are not for everyone'. It's clear: Musk and his cohorts aren't just battling to survive each day, they have a holy mission to achieve their goals.

As a leader, Musk is more a commander-in-chief than a CEO. He's personally ensured the transformation of large numbers of excellent engineers and software developers into vigorous, easily improvising and high-performance commando units. An engineer who left Tesla compares his work to that of the special unit tasked with a secret mission in the movie Apocalypse Now, led by the unorthodox Colonel Kurtz: 'Everything was geared at getting the job done. How you got there, was secondary.'

The parallels between special units and the teams at SpaceX and Tesla are huge:

Deeper meaning
Special units don't just operate towards random goals, they're working on matters bigger than life itself. The comments from people who worked for Musk or still work for him, showcase a continued and deep-seated awareness of the importance of their work. The often superhuman aspirations of the companies create a near-divine passion and dedication.

Ever-changing challenges
Special units face continuously changing challenges. These strongly draw on such personal qualities as decisiveness and improvisational skills. Performing under high pressure gives the ultimate rush. Some even refer to a 'sadomasochistic experience' in this regard, others stick to 'feelings of flow'. Typical of people caught up in the spirit is that they are whipped into a frenzy by 'inexplicable forces' and becoming capable of 'insane peaks in performance'. Despite flow being an individual experience, people are quite capable of enflaming one another. It happens when the spark flies and people push each other to ever-greater heights with their drive and enthusiasm.

Measuring performance on a permanent basis
Special units are constantly given feedback on their performance when obtaining clear-set goals. Each person knows his goals, tasks and action plans. Progress is permanently measured and you give continual accountability for your own performance.

Other people will immediately tackle you on this. It's crystal clear whether or not you're making progress.

Male camaraderie
Finally, there is a strong sense of solidarity. A special unit is a band of brothers. Men who can rely on one another and support each other during battle. In the case of Tesla and SpaceX, this feeling is nurtured from the realization of being an underdog, taking on mighty corporations and governments. Whole nations if need be. 'Every day we realise how vulnerable we are', says one employee. 'It's us against the rest: sink or swim.' That solidarity is also due to Musk's charisma and his setting an example. As the commander-in-chief, he's not just one of the workers—his commitment is authentic.

Spartan

One final remark regarding special units: they dedicate themselves to their mission under Spartan circumstances. Certainly when compared to other high-tech businesses, Musk offers a very sober working environment: old factory buildings and disused production facilities and launching platforms. Engineers involved with rocket launches, used to basking in luxury at their former employer, are housed in locations more resembling a frat house than a hotel. Sometimes it seems that making things more sober is a mission for Musk. For example, he refused to invest in a path between the hangar and the launching platform. 'This left the engineers moving the rocket and its wheeled support structure in the fashion of the ancient Egyptians', biographer Vance writes. 'They laid down a series of wooden planks and rolled the rocket across them, grabbing the last piece of wood from the back and running it forward in a continuous cycle.'

Bare your secrets

By now, Musk may seem reduced to an uncomfortable, directive and detail-oriented nano manager. But there's another side to him: a trusting, sharing and delegating leader.

'Yesterday, there was a wall of Tesla patents in the lobby of our Palo Alto headquarters. That is no longer the case,' he writes to Tesla's employees in June 2014. He decides on an open source approach: other car manufacturers get free access to the technology and knowledge the company has been working on strenuously for years. Those patents were originally intended to prevent competitive brands from copying technological finds, and to then push Tesla out of the market with their massive financial and commercial power. The opposite is true, says Musk: 'Electric car programs at the major manufacturers are small to non-existent. Patents stifle progress and innovation. They entrench the positions of giant corporations and enrich those in the legal profession, rather than the actual inventors.' Whoever wants to use the patented technology in good faith is free to do so. Gladly even, as every contribution to combatting global warming is welcome.

Hyperloop: pneumatic post for people

Another example of sharing and releasing is the ultra-rapid means of transport Musk presented in 2013 under the name Hyperloop. An enormous tube with low air pressure in which vehicles shoot to and fro with speeds reaching 1,200 kilometres per hour. Faster than a passenger jet. This 'pneumatic post for people' is mostly suited to connect cities no farther than 1,000 kilometres' apart. Naturally, the system is powered by solar energy. The goal of this innovative idea is frustrating the plans for a high-speed rail project in

California. 'It would be the slowest bullet train in the world at the highest cost per mile. It's a dead-ending road they're heading down', Musk declared. The high-speed rail project exudes a sense of mediocrity and arrogance that Musk is finding it difficult to stomach. His Hyperloop is estimated to be ten times less expensive and five times faster.

When announcing the Hyperloop, Musk immediately mentions that he has no time to be actively involved in the project. The actual thinking and experimenting he leaves in the hands of a worldwide ecosystem of universities and companies that try, in an open source process, sometimes competing against one another and sometimes cooperating with one another, to further the revolutionary means of transport. Musk is involved as an inspirer and by offering conceptual input, but mostly remains in the background. He lets others have their moment in the sun when it comes to ultrafast transportation.

Musk, the ultimate Wavemaker

'I just enjoy doing things that are useful. Things I believe will improve the future. I want to leave something behind. Look back and be able to say: those things we did back then have really made a difference.' These words of Musk's define the true Wavemakers. Wavemakers are people who stick out because they're dancing half-naked on a hilltop. Who inspire others and imbue them with the enthusiasm to do the same. Wavemakers, with their infectious enthusiasm, play a crucial part in the creation and growth of waves of change.

They influence the way people think and act in different ways. As Superbosses, by drawing in and developing talent. But also by promulgating visionary ideas and connecting people. They also exert influence in their role as opinion leaders, admired at a distance for their cleverness, points of view and achievements.

Hypes of Hollywood allure

That latter role is something Musk was born to. He may not be a natural storyteller like Steve Jobs, but his production achievements create the same kinds of waves of enthusiasm. It makes Musk a welcome guest at conventions and other events. And with his appearance as a role model in the movie *Iron Man* and the main character in *The Simpsons* episode 'The Musk Who Fell To Earth', he's even developed some Hollywood allure.

But perhaps the most important: he's everywhere on social media. He has four million followers on Twitter alone. The power of this medium was proven once more when, on 30 March 2015, he sent a tweet into the world that read: 'Major new Tesla product line -- not a car -- will be unveiled [in one month].' He doesn't say what, just what isn't. His non-message has effect: for a whole month everyone guesses as to what it can be: an electrical airplane, a smartwatch, a network of satellites. Everything passed in review. The hype took on gigantic proportions and Tesla's share prices rose by nearly one billion dollars. Musk revealed the secret on the promised date. The long-expected domestic battery—the Tesla Powerwall—is on its way.

The hype in introducing the new Tesla Model 3 is possibly even bigger: 400,000 people sign on to receive the car in a few years' time. For payment, of course—every wave has its own business model.

MUSK MINI MASTERCLASS:

BE AN INFLUENCER WHO GETS THINGS MOVING

To become an influencer, make sure to acquire talents and bind them to you, inspire others and be a guiding example, like Musk. How can you apply this yourself?

- To what extent are you a Superboss, one that knows how to make talent commit themselves to you? Ask yourself: why should talented people want to commit to you?

- How well do you succeed in letting go of those goals you find important, but can't really find the time for, and leaving them to others? What's stopping you from doing so more often?

- As an influencer, how many people can you reach via traditional and social media (they don't have to number in the millions)? What do you do to stay in touch with your followers on a regular basis?

9

The wave continues

'We will not stop until every car

on the road is electric.'

Elon Musk

Elon Musk is a man of many faces. An optimistic hope bringer, but also a clever techie with excellent know-how. Someone who chases after grand ambitions, but also manifests himself as a pragmatist. A dreamer. A thinker. A doer. And most of all, a go-getter. Because even if at times he skirted the edge, he's still managed to turn everything he's touched into gold. This closing chapter is a retrospective of his Wavemaker qualities. We also take a look at the future: where will Musk be in five years?

When you look at everything he's done so far, you might think Musk must be ancient by now. Nothing could be further from the truth. At age 45, he's still got his life ahead of him. What's more, he's only just begun. It's been ten years since the first (failed) rocket launch. Eight years ago marks the moment the first Tesla Roadster rolled off the assembly line, and four years ago the Tesla Model S, completely self-developed, came into being. Musk runs several exponentially-growing enterprises. Everything he does happens at a killer pace. This bizarre dreamer and thinker of enormous proportions comes up with ideas faster than we can even understand them. He's already thought of the answer before we've even had a chance to ask the question. And as an exceptional entrepreneur, he runs countless businesses and projects. Always on the run, miles ahead of everyone else.

With his invigorating ideas, his peerless decisiveness, guts, choices of the right people and remarkable resilience, Musk overturns moldy corporate sectors with a vengeance. Because his successes didn't come about without a struggle. His performance curve was not a straight upward line, not by far. He's also come through some deep valleys. There were plenty of moments where his mission was in danger of sinking prematurely. To Musk, this was never a reason to throw in the towel. He just straightened his back and went one mile further. Because Musk never quits.

The five waves of the Wavemaker

In this book, we've pegged Musk as a Wavemaker: someone who doesn't just thrive on waves of change, but causes them himself.

1. Waves of hope and expectation
2. Waves of new insights and possibilities
3. Waves of ambitions and intentions
4. Waves of energetic decisiveness
5. Waves of intense cooperation

Wavemakers are at the heart of these waves. They make them swell up and gain in strength. In Musk's case they even become tidal waves, ones that seem a match for the occasional breakwaters: people, groups and organisations that do anything to break the power of the waves of change.

Surging leadership

You could also describe Wavemakers as surging leaders. Not to be confused with serving leaders. Surging leadership means you're capable of getting not just yourself but others moving as well. That you're capable of adapting to changing circumstances. Not by letting yourself float off wherever a passing current takes you, but by also creating swells yourself by way of your own energy. That's how a surging leader is capable of creating new possibilities.

Surging leadership doesn't stop at being dynamic, but also means transcending your contradictions. Musk is a wonderful example of someone who's capable of merging differing elements in his own, unique way. His successful mixture of dreaming, thinking and doing is something we've pointed out before. But the art of combining goes much, much further. He's capable of translating the negative message of man's destruction into an attractive (sort of) possibility of surviving somewhere else in space. And he's not content with it staying a dream, and tries to rationalise and realise his ambition of extraterrestrial life.

While doing so, he's making his indelible mark on reality. His word is law. And yet, Musk demonstrated a remarkably strategic flexibility. Just as effortlessly as he combines 'bossy' and 'non-bossy' elements. He's on top of projects he gives priority. Things that are further removed from his sphere of interest, are relatively easily let go.

Where will Elon Musk be in 2020?

Musk's story is far from over. As we stated at the beginning of the chapter, it is far from over. But we still want to know how it ends. Or better phrased, how it might end. To that end, we've come up with three possible scenarios.

'Musk is the Leonardo da Vinci

of the 21st century.'

Scenario 1: Musk rules the world

The ultimate success scenario. A year or five from now, life centres around all the activities and enterprises started by Musk. We leave our solar-powered house in our Tesla to go to the Hyperloop station, which will take us to the nearest SpaceX airport. The rest of the family's waiting there to spend a wonderful weekend on a tropical island. In a state-of-the-art, electrically-powered and exceptionally quiet SpaceX airplane, naturally, which takes off and lands vertically. Waiting for boarding, you eat a nutritious and 3D-printed meal. And while doing so, you make good use of the fast SpaceX satellite connections. Probable? Not really. But don't underestimate Musk. Say it does become reality—Musk will instantly become Thomas Edison, Henry Ford and Steve Jobs combined. The Leonardo da Vinci of the 21st century. He's managed impossible things before. If his dreams come true, he will soon be an unequalled tycoon who owns important, but largely ignored, economic sectors.

A possible variation of this scenario: Musk doesn't continue solo, but combines forces with powerful parties such as Apple or Google. The first possibility has already been the subject of many discussions for years now: Apple could use a little creative input after the dull years since Steve Job's passing. Musk can do that. Reversely, Musk has a continuing need for capital and Apple—just like Google, we might add—has no shortage of that. A marriage of convenience between two parties who don't really appreciate each other and have spent their time thus far in stealing each other's talent? It's not something that can be entirely dismissed.

Scenario 2: MASA
Musk does the same thing he did when starting out as an entrepreneur. It begins with a number of failures. The promised number of Teslas fall far short of the actual result. The reason is production errors, mainly caused by incorrectly programmed robots and wildcat strikes by dissatisfied employees. The management is not equipped for its tasks, which is unsurprising, as running a start-up is quite simply in a different ballpark than running a major production company.

Musk makes the best of a bad bargain, and sells the automobile section to a big German brand for big bucks. Just like in his internet days. The energy department and the battery factory are taken over by an Asian concern. In both cases Musk remains involved as CEO to guard the courses.

What does Musk do with all this money? He focuses 100 per cent on realising his dream of going to Mars. The American space agency NASA is rechristened to MASA, with the M of Mars and Musk. For Musk dominates international aerospace: he's setting the pace and determining the next move.

Selling his other businesses garners him a lot of criticism from disappointed fans. Musk tries to quell the negative emotions by pointing out that his goal was to increase the environmental awareness of car brands, which they now are. His task is done. Same thing applies to solar energy. And for the rest: bite me. Musk does whatever he wants. And he wants to go to Mars. To live there and to die there.

Scenario 3: Musk explodes or implodes
A somewhat grim, but certainly not implausible scenario concludes our trilogy. The years of expending his strength takes its toll. After years of stress and sleepless nights, Musk's health is in a very dangerous state: he dies of a heart attack. Or, after a night partying, dead on his feet, he crashes his Tesla into a tree. Exit scene. Not just for Musk, but for all his companies, too. Because without the Wavemaker to run them, they fall apart. Musk will forever be an icon taken away too soon. He says his last goodbyes with a final explosion: his ashes are launched into space.

Another, possible variation: Musk implodes. After all those years of projecting his energy outwards, he looks inward, exploring his inner universe. With his skills, this could easily lead to groundbreaking ideas in medicine, psychology and even spirituality. The cause is the school he started in secret in 2015, which he intended his own sons to go to as well. This school, Ad Astra—Latin for 'to the stars'—offers children everything he lacked himself in his own school days. A safe environment, where children can fully develop all their talents. He teaches there himself. And you could say he's also teaching himself, in a manner of speaking. He reinvents himself. He becomes more social and focuses completely on the new generation Musk 2.0. Because they are his real back-up for humanity.

What can you do?

We started writing this book out of our fascination with the incredible successes of this visionary, inventor and entrepreneur. We've been able to explain these successes by using five success principles. And this opens the door on a different, much more important goal: the realisation that each and every one of us can make the difference in the things we do.

To become a Wavemaker yourself, you really don't need to aim for Mars. There's only one Elon Musk. But Wavemakers come in all shapes and sizes. There are, without doubt, countless possibilities in your own life and working environment to start making waves, to have an impact.

And if it's not you, it may be your children or your friend's children. Because what about the next story? There was a newspaper story in late May that an inventor, inspired by Nikola Tesla, had created a device that can extract electricity from the air. He says he was born to change the world with his inventions. 'From day one on this planet, I knew I was put here for a reason. And that reason is to invent.' The name of this inventor? Max Loughan, barely 13 years old. The wave goes on.

Afterword

During the creation of this book, I became fascinated by Elon Musk's story of adventure, fueled by the energetic talks I had with Hans and Patrick. But, with all respect to his achievements, you, a person or entrepreneur, might think twice on changing tack after reading this book, and go on 'Elon Musk style'. Personally, I'd advise against it. Even though everything he's achieved is worthy of praise, the price he paid for this success is steep. Maybe his approach is typically American, but I think his formula of success is lacking a little European 'chill'. There's a reason why entrepreneurs such as Danae Ringelmann, founder of crowdfunding Indiegogo, say in public that when American entrepreneurs, especially those from Silicon Valley, rule the world, it may become more exciting, but certainly not more fun.

Musk may have a set of unique skills, the question remains whether his lifestyle offers enough room for reflection, quiet and simply 'being'. I'm also curious whether or not his technical approach to problems is always that effective. Does that approach leave enough room for the less rational aspects that are involved in solving human and social issues? After all, life is simply not just a matter of practicality. And us humans are not consistently logical creatures. Far from it.

By the time you're reading this book, Elon Musk's expedition has probably entered its next phase. Will he succeed or not? This is a question occupying a great many people. You could equally wonder whether success is finite. I think it is. In fact, I know it is. After all, everything in life is subject to processes of growth, stagnation and decay. But why is this insight important? Because even if the next three rockets crash and he still can't manage to ramp up Tesla's production capabilities, the impact of his actions is still enormous. Elon Musk's goals are to put space travel on the map and create sustainable mobility and energy generation. Because he's worried about the future of the world and humanity. The achievements he's realised already fulfil most of his goals. Others follow his example and are rushing to renew important economic sectors. They are inspired by his ideas and further them. Or they line up in droves to follow his example. Musk has already succeeded in his mission: the wave has been set in motion.

Martijn Arets,
Leader of the Crowd Expedition and expert in the field of the sharing economy.

Acknowledgements

The period between the fledgling start and the eventual publication of a book may take years. This was not the case with *Musk Mania*. This book wrote itself. While collecting information on Wavemakers, Elon Musk's name popped up constantly. We became fascinated and decided to dedicate a chapter to him in our as-of-yet unpublished book on *Wavemakers*. That chapter unexpectedly grew into *Musk Mania*.

Many people supported us and gave us advice while writing this book. We want to thank a few people by name. Firstly, Isabel Timmers: she acted as our constant reader, refining texts, eliminating less important passages and helping us with some surprising insights. She has earned the title of co-author.

Martijn Arets, who wrote the afterword, deserves our thanks for his knowledge and enthusiasm during the research into Wavemakers. Vivianne Smiggels drew the design for the book cover—with no experience, yet spot on. Eva de Valk, Silicon Valley expert and author of the eponymous book, has our gratitude for her feedback and the foreword. We would also like to thank Phil Larsson (SpaceX), Anton van der Wulp (Tesla Motors) and Dirk Ahlborn (Hyperloop Transportation Technologies).

Our major thanks also extend to the energetic crew of Vakmedianet: Neeltje de Kroon, Freek Talsma, Astrid Geraats, Laurens Molegraaf, Monique Krol and Anneke van

Dijk. You made this book happen with peerless enthusiasm, improvisational talent and vigour.

We dedicate Musk Mania to our children: Sebas, Joran and Cas. They are our hope bringers of the future. They ask the important questions and chase after huge ambitions. They are the Wavemakers of tomorrow.

Hans and Patrick, June 2016

Sources

We consulted dozens of books, hundreds of videos and thousands of articles and blogs in writing *Musk Mania*. The following are the most essential sources. For more background information, visit www.muskmania.com. There you will also find blogs by the authors. In the future, we will also share updates on the first edition of the book which was published in July 2016 in The Netherlands by Vakmedianet.

Books

- Diamandis, Peter H. & Steve Kotler (2015). *Bold: How to Go Big, Create Wealth and Impact the World.* New York: Simon & Schuster.
- Downes, Larry & Pablo Nunes (2014). *Big Bang Disruption: Strategy in the Age of Devastating Innovation.* Londen: Penguin.
- Finkelstein, Sydney (2016). *Superbosses: How Exceptional Leaders Master the Flow of Talent.* Londen: Portfolio Penguin.
- Ginneken, Jaap van (2012). *Het enthousiasmevirus.* Amsterdam/Antwerpen: Business Contact.
- Grant, Adam (2016). *Originals: How Non-conformists Change the World.* Londen: WH Allen.
- Kolind, Lars & Jacob Bøtter (2012). *Unboss.* Deventer: Vakmedianet.
- Lane, Randall (2014). *You Only Have To Be Right Once: The Unprecedented Rise of the Instant Tech Billionaires.* Londen: Portfolio Penguin.
- Newport, Carl (2016). *Diep werk: Werken met aandacht in een wereld vol afleiding.* Amsterdam/Antwerpen: Business Contact.

- Snow, Shane (2014). *Smart Cuts: De snelste weg naar succes.* Amsterdam: Bruna Uitgevers.
- Thiel, Peter (2014). *Zero to One: Creëer de toekomst.* Amsterdam/Antwerpen: Business Contact.
- Tjan, Anthony K., Richard J. Harrington & Tsun-Yan Hsieh (2012). *Heart, Smarts, Guts and Luck: What It Takes To Be an Entrepreneur and Build a Great Business.* Boston: Harvard Business Review Press.
- Valk, Eva de (2014). *Silicon Valley: Waar de toekomst wordt gemaakt.* Amsterdam: Lebowski Publishers.
- Vance, Ashlee (2016). *Elon Musk: Hoe de topman van Space X en Tesla onze toekomst vormgeeft.* Amsterdam: Bruna Uitgevers.
- Vorst, Roland van der (2009). *Hoop: Hoe we door de toekomst worden verleid.* Amsterdam: Nieuw Amsterdam Uitgevers.

Articles and blogs

- www.businessinsider.com
- www.elonmusknews.org
- www.glassdoor.com
- www.inc.com
- www.indeed.com
- www.quora.com
- www.spaceX.com
- www.technewsworld.com
- www.tesla.com
- www.theverge.com
- www.waitbutwhy.com

Videos

Elon Musk: The mind behind Tesla, SpaceX, SolarCity (zoek op: TED, Elon Musk). Interview of Chris Anderson (TED) with Elon Musk: www.youtube.com/watch?v=3Zfpv4DzXB8.

Elon Musks Vision for the Future (search for: Elon Musks Vision for the Future). Musk at his finest, interviewed by his friend Steve Jurvetson. www.youtube.com/watch?v=SVk1hb0ZOrE. Also available as a podcast.

A report of the legendary CRS-8 mission, in which the Falcon 9 rocket landed on the drone ship Of Course I Still Love You on the 8 April 2016 (search for CRS-8 DragonHosted Webcast, via SpaceX's YouTube channel): www.youtube.com/watch?v=7pUAydjne5M.

Tesla Motors - The Future of Electric Cars. www.youtube.com/watch?v=Y7IqFOsBOb8.

Elon Musk tours the SpaceX Complex: www.youtube.com/watch?v=1nCCjojCl14.

Wavemakers

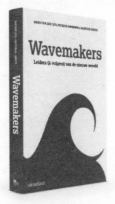

Changing the world by doing things ten (or more!) times faster, better and cheaper. Putting up a fight with established forces and realising ground-breaking innovations. Challenging the status quo and casually pushing aside certainties and replacing them with your own logics and rules you chose. Always being one step ahead of the rest of the world. Welcome in the world of the Wavemakers!

In Spring 2018, we will publish *Wavemakers*, the results of a research project that took several years—the brainchild of Patrick Davidson and Hans van der Loo, together with Martijn Arets. The authors have spent the last few years interviewing dozens of Wavemakers in the Netherlands and abroad, getting to the heart of their leadership, the way they behave and how they manage to convey their behaviour onto others. *Wavemakers* is furthermore based on treasure troves of wisdom, archive cases chock-full of research results and, above all, thousands of minutes of home-made movie material. *Musk Mania*, which features Elon Musk, is the first publication from the research project.

Like to know more, visit
www.wavemakers.info.
For more information on Elon Musk,
visit www.muskmania.com.

wavemakers